Colonial
APPLIQUÉ

Colonial APPLIQUÉ

INSPIRATIONS FROM EARLY AMERICA

SHEILA WINTLE

Martingale
& COMPANY

Bothell, Washington

CREDITS

President ∿ Nancy J. Martin
CEO ∿ Daniel J. Martin
Publisher ∿ Jane Hamada
Editorial Director ∿ Mary V. Green
Editorial Project Manager ∿ Tina Cook
Design and Production Manager ∿ Stan Green
Technical Editor ∿ Jane Townswick
Copy Editor ∿ Ellen Balstad
Illustrators ∿ Laurel Strand, Lisa McKenney
Photographer ∿ Brent Kane
Cover and Text Design ∿ Rohani Design

That Patchwork Place is an imprint of Martingale & Company.

MISSION STATEMENT
We are dedicated to providing quality products and service by working together to inspire creativity and to enrich the lives we touch.

Colonial Appliqué: Inspirations from Early America
© 2000 by Sheila Wintle

Martingale & Company
PO Box 118
Bothell, WA 98041-0118 USA
www.patchwork.com

Printed in China
05 04 03 02 01 00   6 5 4 3 2 1

Library of Congress Cataloging-in-Publication Data

Wintle, Sheila.
    Colonial appliqué : inspirations from early America / Sheila Wintle.
        p. cm.
    ISBN 1-56477-298-5
    1. Appliqué—Patterns. 2. Quilts—Design. 3. Decoration and ornament—Plant forms. 4. Coverlets—United States—History—17th century. I Title.

TT779.W56 2000
746.46'041'097309032—dc21

00-038004

DEDICATION

To my parents, Mary and Lloyd Wintle, with thanks from a grateful daughter.

To my sister, Marilyn, for reminding me, "It's just quilts."

And to all my family for their support and patience.

ACKNOWLEDGMENTS

Ms. Celia Oliver, Curator of Textile Collections, Shelburne Museum, Shelburne, Vermont, for sharing her knowledge of bed ruggs, and Ms. Sharon Green, Assistant Manager of Collection, Shelburne Museum, Shelburne, Vermont for research assistance.

Thank you to my dear friend, Sandi Pope, of Ottawa, Ontario for her generous help in preparing quilts and giving encouragement.

Thanks to my mother, Mary, for the excellent job of hand quilting and for binding the quilts.

CONTENTS

The Projects

INTRODUCTION

The opening sentence of Charles Dickens' novel *David Copperfield* reads, "I am born." This simple statement reflects the feeling I experienced when I first encountered the fascinating world of quilts and quiltmaking. As a self-taught quilter, I wanted to try everything. I learned a lot about patterns and design from studying old quilts, which were masterpieces of both color and technique. Two books, Ruby McKim's *101 Patchwork Patterns* and Carter Houck's *American Quilts and How to Make Them* were especially helpful to me. Carter Houck's book contained many examples of the finest vintage quilts and listed the museums where they were located. This gave me the idea to seek out other museums and study their textile collections.

While researching various vintage textiles in addition to quilts, I discovered colonial bed ruggs, which are Early American cousins of the quilt. Made primarily in the area of New England, these

Hannah Johnson, American, 1770–1848, Connecticut, United States, bed rug, wool, plain weave; embroidered with wool yarns in looped running stitches, cut from form pile, 1796, 249.4 x 246.1 cm. Restricted gift of the Needlework and Textile Guild of Chicago, 1944.27 © 2000, The Art Institute of Chicago. All rights reserved.

wonderful linen and wool textiles overflow with lovely, large-scale flowers, vases, vines, and leaves like the one in the photo at left. Only brief mention of Colonial bed ruggs can be found in various reference books, and only about seventy-five of these beautiful bed coverings remain in existence today. Many bed ruggs were made in Connecticut from about 1722 to 1833, along the more settled areas of the Connecticut River. These examples are very rare and highly prized by both collectors and museum curators throughout the world.

Some bed ruggs were made with a darning stitch on a plain linen background, with the wool stitching covering the total surface, while others were constructed with a loop pile. The colors used in bed ruggs were extremely vibrant shades of green, blue, and gold, often on dark backgrounds.

Very little is known about the origins of the designs or how the makers of bed ruggs obtained their patterns, but many recurring motifs point to a distinctively English influence. One example of this type of design element is a stylized Tree of Life. Another is a small, squatty vase that was used to replace more elaborate, rooted shapes in some of the bed ruggs. You can see this type of vase in the "High Style" quilt shown on page 104. Another clue to the English heritage of bed ruggs is the carnation, which, in some bed ruggs, takes on the appearance of a Scottish thistle. Even the word "rugg" carries the British spelling. However, the New England bed rugg is a truly American product. As I delved more deeply into researching these fascinating textiles, I quickly realized that with just a few minor changes, it would be easy to adapt motifs such as these to appliqué quilts, and they would be both beautiful and fun to stitch.

As a quilting teacher, I often hear remarks like "If only I could draw." The full-size, ready-to-use patterns in this book will enable you to make thirteen quilts in the floral style of the colonial bed ruggs. And you can even go one step further. Choosing the "mix-and-match" option will put the design process at your fingertips and allow you to create your own original quilt designs. All of the projects feature motifs and design elements that are compatible in both scale and style, which makes it easy to choose elements from different projects and combine them in new and exciting ways. Whether you decide to make quilts as they are shown, or come up with unique designs of your own, I hope you enjoy the simplicity and fun of *Colonial Appliqué* and delight in expressing your own creativity in your quilts.

Sheila Wintle

TOOLS AND SUPPLIES

To make the experience of appliquéing more enjoyable and to improve the quality of your stitching, it is important to use high-quality supplies. The following tools, notions, and supplies have worked well for me, and I hope they will do the same for you.

Eyeglasses

Many of us are at that phase of life when the print in the telephone book seems to grow increasingly smaller. If this sounds familiar, my suggestion is to take your appliqué work with you the next time you visit an eye-care professional. While your vision is being checked, look through the refractors at your appliqué work. You should be able to see the fabric, thread for thread, and your appliqué, stitch for stitch. I own a pair of eyeglasses that contains only the prescription I need for stitching. While these eyeglasses offer a limited range of vision, I can see both my appliqué work and computer monitor easily. The ability to see well at close range will improve the quality of your stitches tremendously.

Proper Lighting

A good light source is equally as important as good eyeglasses. Now widely available at quilt shops, the Ott Lite True-Color lamp produces such a high-quality light that it is really like sewing in sunshine. Whatever type of light source you use, position it so that you can avoid sewing in the shadow of your own hand, which can affect the quality of your stitches. Beware of eyestrain as well. If your eyes ache, take a break from stitching. If necessary, check with your eyecare professional for appropriate eye drops to soothe them. Appliquéing will be more fun if you are comfortable.

Needles

Richard Hemming, large-eyed Milliner's needles in size #10 or #11 are long, which makes them work well for basting and needle-turn appliqué. Since these needles can bend occasionally, I usually purchase a few packages rather than just one at a time. That way I can occasionally use a fresh needle and make sure that I'm always working with a needle that has a good, sharp point. For very delicate stitching, I recommend size #12 John James Sharps, which have a thin shank and a very small eye. To keep any appliqué needle sharp, I like to stick the point into an emery strawberry attached to a tomato pincushion, press tightly, and rotate the needle to sharpen it. If a barb develops on the point of a needle, the emery will help remove it.

Threads

To be sure that your appliqué stays in place and does not become unstitched, use high-quality threads. Mettler sewing thread, size 50/3, is fine, durable, and comes in a wide range of colors. If you prefer a finer weight thread, use Mettler embroidery thread, size 60/2, which has a smaller range of colors. Silk thread is also lovely to work with but it is more expensive and not as readily available.

Match the color of the thread you use as closely as possible to the fabric in your appliqué. When you cut a length of thread, always knot the end you cut. Thread consists of three individual strands that are twisted together. By using the thread as it comes off the spool, you are working with the thread direction rather than going against its twist.

For basting thread, I recommend using YLI Basting Thread. This soft cotton thread comes on very economical, 800-yard spools and lasts a long time. It is single-ply thread and it will break before your stitches become distorted. It is also excellent for basting quilt layers.

For piecing and sewing construction, I use a neutral, 100 percent–cotton thread, size 50/3. Off-white thread is good for light colors, medium gray for medium colors, and black for very dark fabrics. Mettler thread is available on large spools, which is more economical for this type of general sewing.

Needle Threaders

To keep your stitching stress-free, a needle threader can be helpful. I use a Clover needle threader with two wires—one for needles that have regular size eyes and the other for needles with very fine eyes. You may also find it helpful to cut an angle the end of the thread that will go through the eye of the needle.

Thimbles

I have a large variety of thimbles, with different ones for different tasks. Some days my hands feel a little puffy and I need a large thimble. On other days, that same thimble might fall off my finger and I can use a smaller one. Following years of quilting, the joints in my fingers have become enlarged and one thimble that I have especially enjoyed is my Comfort Thimble. It is made of soft, lightweight, molded plastic so that my joints do not ache from wearing it. It is best suited for appliqué rather than quilting. For hand quilting, I use a more heavy-duty metal thimble with a raised metal lip that prevents the needle from slipping. There again, I have different sizes for all occasions. Choose whatever thimble works well for you.

Scissors

High-quality scissors are important for cutting out appliqués easily. Look for scissors with blades that are not too long so that you have better control over cutting small seam allowances. I use a pair of Clover Patchwork Scissors with a serrated blade that holds fabric and makes smooth cuts. Whatever brand of scissors you choose, use them only for cutting fabric.

Pins

I like to use a few fine glass-headed pins to hold appliqué elements in place on a background square. However, with my half-basting technique, it isn't necessary to do a lot of pinning. If you use pins, make sure that they do not displace your appliqués.

Marking Pencils

I use a variety of pencils for marking a project, including white, silver, or fine-line mechanical pencils. The most important thing is to sharpen your pencil frequently so that you can mark a consistently fine line. It is not unusual to use up an entire pencil when marking an appliqué project! When the seam allowances are turned under, your marking lines should no longer be visible. Before you mark the appliqué shapes for a project, test the pencil you want to use on scraps of your fabrics. If any color rubs off or leaves a permanent stain, choose a different marking pencil.

Template Material

For tracing appliqué shapes, use clear template plastic. It is firm, easy to mark and cut, and you can see fabrics through it, which is helpful for positioning prints effectively in an appliqué project.

FABRIC SAVVY

I use only 100 percent–cotton fabric that has been prewashed and resized with spray sizing. When you purchase fabric, look at the edge as it lies on the bolt, and pay special attention to the amount of fraying. Look for fabrics that are firmly woven. There is nothing worse than having a point fray when you are ready to appliqué it. Gather the fabric in your hand and hold it firmly. Remember that this is what you will do to it while you are appliquéing.

Once you select your fabric, launder it to see whether it holds up well without a lot of raveling. I have had the experience of discovering that a background fabric was unsuitable after washing it. The fabric was too flimsy and would not have withstood the necessary handling involved in making a quilt. It would have been easier on my budget if I had followed my own advice and auditioned a fat quarter of the fabric. To launder cotton fabrics, use Orvus paste soap, cold water, and a white basin. A white basin allows you to determine whether a fabric contains a lot of extra dye that needs to be rinsed out, and it also makes it easy to see when the fabric has been rinsed clear. After you launder a fabric in this way, it is ready to use in a quilt. Dry cotton fabric in a dryer until it is just damp, which will make it easier to press. Just before you press, mist the wrong side of the fabric with spray sizing to restore its quilt-shop freshness and to create a crisp finish.

CHOOSING A COLOR PALETTE

Deciding on a color palette can be the most fun part of any project, but when you are faced with a quilt shop full of fabulous choices, it can also be a bit overwhelming (or even stressful). Color is a very personal and instinctive thing. There are no rules—you either like a color or you don't. My suggestion is to keep it simple, and keep in mind that a beautiful palette can consist of twenty fabrics or just a few. Read through the following discussion of different fabric types, and remember that the most important thing is that you like the way your fabric choices look together.

Large-Scale Prints

The quilt designs in this book are large and have plenty of space for large-scale prints. My starting point is to look for a large print that contains lots of colors and create a color palette with the colors in it, as shown in this traditional grouping.

Choose large-scale prints for some of the appliqués.

Abstract, large-scale prints sometimes lend themselves to a more contemporary color palette, like the following example. One good thing to remember about large-scale prints is that they are great for large places. You can see an example of this in the "Flowing Leaf" quilt on page 49, where I used a large-scale, abstract black print for the leaves and scalloped border.

Pull colors from a print to create a color palette.

Sometimes a large-scale print seems visually overwhelming or contains a lot of empty spaces or very light areas in the print. If you want to use a fabric like this one, be aware that you might need to cut it into smaller pieces to use it effectively in a quilt, or select another, more evenly printed fabric. Remember that in a quilt shop you see fabric in long, uncut lengths on a bolt rather than in small appliqué shapes. In "Asters and Daisies" on page 94, I used a large-scale print in the piecing of the Dogtooth border. This particular print was not suitable for individual appliqué shapes because it conflicted with the shapes themselves, but it worked very well for the pieced border.

Cut visually overwhelming prints like this into small pieces.

Darks, Mediums, and Lights

It is important to include a selection of light, medium, and dark fabrics in your color palette so that all of the colors stand out rather than blend together. For example, leaves in nature have a light top and a dark underside, with a medium middle. In addition to a variety of color values, include prints, tone-on-tone, and textured fabrics for a well-rounded color palette.

Use a variety of fabric textures for leaves.

> TIP: If there is one fabric you do not care for, remove it from your palette and select another, or it will always be the element you see first in the finished quilt.

Accent Fabrics

A fabric that adds a touch of visual emphasis to your color palette is an effective accent fabric. In "Rose Ring" on page 41, for example, notice the touch of somber gold in the large print. I decided that the ring area and flower centers were just the right places for small amounts of this accent color. Try a variegated or shaded accent fabric, as I did for the large leaves in "Pomegranates" on page 61.

> TIP: In *Colonial Appliqué*, you do not have to shade realistically. You can make your appliqué pieces any color you wish, such as purple leaves and pink circles. Be creative!

Backgrounds

The most important part of a color palette is the background fabric. It should receive special consideration, because it sets the tone for your quilt. The background fabric you choose does not need to be a solid color. Look for printed fabric that has texture and a firm weave, and think about how your palette of appliqué fabrics will look on it. Textured prints, like the examples shown below, will enhance your appliqué design. For example, in "Pomegranates" on page 61, notice the checkerboard border and the texture of the checked background fabric in the center block. And in the "High Style" quilt on page 104, I used a tone-on-tone, large leaf print as the background fabric to coordinate with the large leaves in the appliqué design.

Background fabrics need not only be light colors, either. Consider using a medium-value fabric, such as the gold background of "Fleur-de-Lys" on page 77. This medium-value background color creates a calm surface, blending color and pattern. A dark background fabric makes vibrant colors shine, and a bright background, such as the yellow fabric in "Carnation and Acanthus Leaf" on page 34, gives a quilt lots of personality. Using a very light or dark background creates a strong contrast between different sections of a quilt and less of a blending effect. Consider fabrics with one-way directional patterns, and see how this type of print would affect your overall design. The "Rose Ring" quilt on page 41 has a directional print in the background, but because the texture is very light, it is not distracting, either to the appliqué or border areas. If the one-way direction of a print is very strong, it can strike a discordant note. Using this type of fabric can also mean that you may need to purchase extra fabric and cut it to accommodate the directional factor.

Consider using textured prints for the background.

GETTING READY FOR APPLIQUÉ

his section explains the techniques that I have developed for my half-baste, needle-turn method of appliqué, including template preparation, marking fabric, making bias stems and perfect circles, half-basting appliqué shapes, and using the center block diagrams as a guide to stitching the center blocks.

Making Templates

Before you begin tracing pattern pieces, note that there are dashed lines in the patterns on edges that will lie underneath another appliqué shape; another portion of the design will cover these edges when you get to the preconstruction stage. The amount of overlap between appliqué shapes will be ¼". Solid lines indicate the edges that will be basted.

Dashed lines indicate edges
to be overlapped.

Using a fine-tip permanent marker, trace the appliqué pattern pieces onto clear template plastic. On each template include the name of the pattern piece and the number you will need to cut of that piece. If you will need to cut any pieces in the reversed position, label the template with the word *reversed* or the letter *R* and indicate the number to

cut in the reversed position. Do not add any seam allowances to appliqué templates.

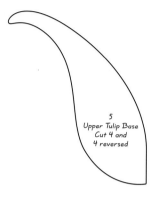

5
Upper Tulip Base
Cut 4 and
4 reversed

Place all of the templates that make up each flower or leaf unit in a small, resealable plastic bag. Then place all of the templates for your entire project into a larger resealable bag. This will help avoid the confusion that can come from working with a multitude of templates at one time. Be as accurate as possible in tracing templates, as there is nothing more frustrating than an appliqué shape that does not fit into a design properly.

> TIP: Appliqué is more portable when pieces are basted in place on the background fabric. You can stitch in a doctor's office, in a sports arena, or take a bit of handwork with you on a vacation. With basted shapes, you can avoid the problems of stabbing your fingers on pins or getting threads tangled around pins.

Marking and Cutting Appliqués

On the right side of the fabric, use a marking pen or pencil for fabric to mark around each appliqué template needed for your project. As you cut out each shape, use the "eyeball" method to add a ¼" seam allowance to all sides. In other words, cut the seam allowances freehand without measuring or marking them first. The more appliqué pattern pieces you cut out, the better you will get at estimating this distance. Be sure to leave adequate space between appliqué pieces, but be conservative in your fabric usage. Leave ½" to ⅝" between each appliqué piece so that it will be easy to add the ¼" seam allowances when you cut out the pieces.

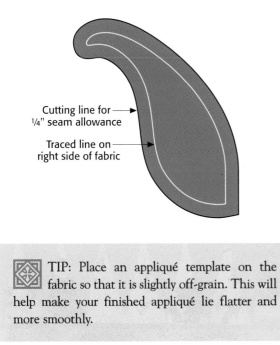

Cutting line for ¼" seam allowance

Traced line on right side of fabric

TIP: Place an appliqué template on the fabric so that it is slightly off-grain. This will help make your finished appliqué lie flatter and more smoothly.

Clipping is very important when working with appliqué shapes. Make clips approximately three-fourths of the way into the seam allowance, at ½" intervals around the entire shape that is to be appliquéd. Do not clip outer points or they will fray unnecessarily. Clip only seam allowance areas that will be turned under the appliqué; it is not necessary to clip seam allowances that will be overlapped by another appliqué shape.

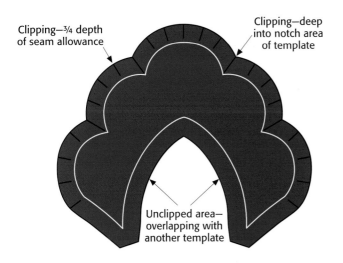

Clipping—¾ depth of seam allowance

Clipping—deep into notch area of template

Unclipped area—overlapping with another template

Bias Stems and Vines

All of the stems and vines in this book are made from bias strips that are cut ⅞" wide. From a corner of your stem or vine fabric, rotary cut a 45° angle from the selvage edge, establishing the bias grain. The lengths of stems and vines vary from project to project, so it is best to wait until after you have cut all of the appliqué shapes and positioned them on the background fabric to cut your bias strips. Next, measure the length needed for each vine or stem in your project, and cut the number of bias strips you need in those lengths.

To prepare a stem or vine for appliqué, place a bias strip on a pressing surface with the right side of the fabric facing down. Use spray sizing to dampen the fabric. Fold one third of the bias strip lengthwise, toward the middle, and press the fold. Leaving the pressed bias strip in place, fold the remaining third of the bias strip over the pressed portion, and press the second fold. You will have a three-fold stem that is ready to appliqué—no basting necessary!

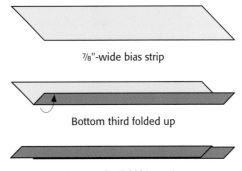

⅞"-wide bias strip

Bottom third folded up

Prepared 3-fold bias strip

Perfect Circles

I like the old-fashioned way of preparing circles for appliqué. Mark whatever size circle you need on the fabric for your project and cut it out, adding a ¼" seam allowance. Do a row of gathering stitches inside the seam allowance, all the way around the circle. From an index card, cut a paper circle that is exactly the finished size you need without a seam allowance. Place the paper circle on the wrong side of the fabric circle. Pull gently on the gathering stitches, gathering the fabric neatly around the paper circle. Knot and clip the thread, lightly misting the wrong side of the prepared circle with spray sizing. Press the fabric circle to create a crisp fold that is easy to stitch. All of the circles in this book are fairly large and easy to appliqué when they are prepared in this way. Remove the paper circle from the fabric circle just before you are ready to stitch it on a block.

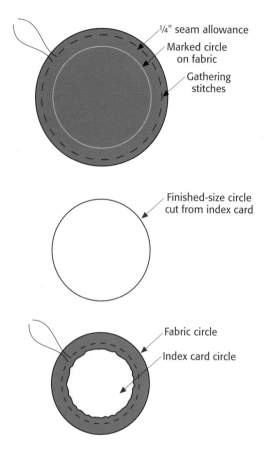

¼" seam allowance

Marked circle on fabric

Gathering stitches

Finished-size circle cut from index card

Fabric circle

Index card circle

Half-Basting and Preconstructing Appliqués

The half-baste, needle-turn method of appliqué involves turning under and basting portions of the seam allowances of each appliqué shape with a Milliner's needle. Seam allowances in more difficult areas of the appliqués, such as leaf or petal points or the notch at the top of a heart, remain unbasted. For this method, begin by turning under the seam allowance along the turning lines, or marked pattern lines, on each shape. Work with the right side

of the shape facing up. Use a long Milliner's needle and YLI Basting Thread to baste the seam allowance in place. When you reach a point or notch, make a short clip into the seam allowance near each side and leave this area unbasted.

After you finish basting the seam allowances of the individual appliqué shapes, press the shapes lightly to create a crisp, easy-to-stitch fold; then group them into units. (Some shapes are separate and are not part of a unit. Refer to specific project directions for more details.) Follow the numerical sequence indicated on the pattern pieces to baste, or preconstruct, the individual shapes together. Use YLI Basting Thread and a Milliner's needle. Leave the thread unknotted so that it will be easy to remove the basting stitches later, after all the appliqué work is complete.

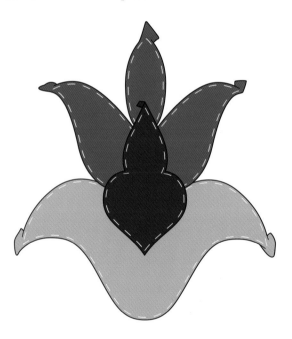

TIP: Fill your needle with several basting stitches at a time before pulling the thread through the fabric. This will make the basting process go more quickly. You can also use a long thread and baste one shape after another continuously, leaving an inch of thread between shapes as a spacer.

Preparing a Center Block

All of the center blocks in this book have a finished size of 24" x 24" except for two quilts. The reason for the difference is explained in the instructions for those quilts. Follow these basic steps to prepare the center block for all of the projects.

1. With a rotary cutter, ruler, and mat, remove the selvages from the edges of your fabrics. Measure each side of a 25" square separately. If your ruler is too short, make a mark to indicate the length of the ruler and extend the ruler to reach 25" on each side. Use the rotary cutter, ruler, and mat to cut out the center block from a single layer of your yardage.

2. Press diagonal, horizontal, and vertical folds in the center block. These lines will provide guidance for placing the appliqué pieces on the fabric. If your pressed lines fade, it is easy to press them again.

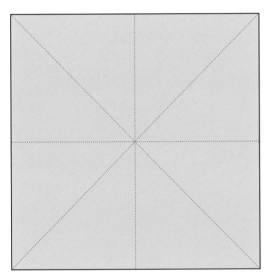

25" x 25" cut center block

3. Mark, cut, and half-baste the appliqué shapes. Following the numerical stitching sequences indicated on the pattern pieces, preconstruct the appliqué units. Pay special attention to how the various appliqué units and shapes fit together, and watch for places where one design element goes over or under another.

4. Pin the half-basted and preconstructed units, and the individual appliqué shapes, stems, or vines, in position on the center block. Use the center block diagram as a placement guide. Refer to the sections that follow to pin or baste and stitch the elements of the design in place by hand or machine appliqué.

Tulip and Thorn Leaf Center Block Diagram

5. Finally, there are many schools of thought about cutting away the background fabric from underneath appliqué shapes after the stitching is completed. Cutting away the background fabric does remove an extra layer of fabric, which makes hand quilting easier. With large-scale appliqué, I prefer to leave the background fabric intact because it would be greatly weakened by trimming. If your stitching ever came undone, you might have to repair a large hole in your quilt.

HAND APPLIQUÉ

*T*he traditional appliqué stitch is simple to do, and it holds appliqués securely to the background fabric. Follow these easy steps to do lovely hand appliqué on all of your *Colonial Appliqué* projects.

Starting a Thread

The thread length you use can vary depending on the size of the piece you are stitching, but a 14" length of thread generally works well. Tie a secure knot in a length of thread. Tack the knotted end to the background fabric under the appliqué shape, tacking a bit in from the edge to ensure that the thread tail is not visible in your finished work.

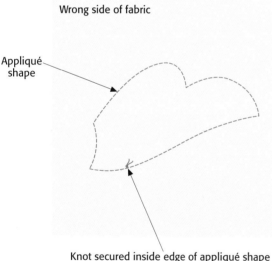

Wrong side of fabric

Appliqué shape

Knot secured inside edge of appliqué shape on wrong side of background fabric

TIP: A longer thread can fray from being pulled through fabric repeatedly. If your thread frays, simply tie off the thread and start a new one.

Stitch Length

Bring the needle up from the wrong side of the background fabric, through all layers, into the folded edge of the appliqué. Bring the needle out of the fold and insert it back into the background fabric, directly beside the appliqué shape. Bring the needle up through the background fabric approximately $\frac{1}{8}$" away, and catch the folded edge of the appliqué again, as shown.

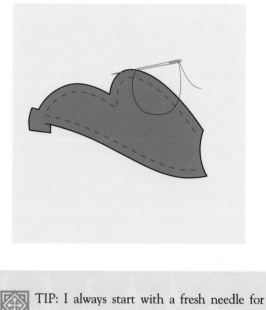

TIP: I always start with a fresh needle for each project and a new thread for each appliqué shape.

Your appliqué stitches should all be the same length, and the distance between them should be less than $\frac{1}{8}$", so that the appliqué shapes will be stitched securely in place. After you take each stitch, give the thread a slight tug to add a little tension and to keep the appliqué securely in place. You will have smooth creases to work with on the basted edges. For unbasted areas that need to be needle turned, such as points of petals and leaves, use a long Milliner's needle as your turning tool. Stitch right to the point of your marked turning line; then use the needle tip to turn the seam allowance right at the point. If there is too much fabric in the seam allowance, trim it to a scant ¼". Otherwise there will be a thick bump of fabric at the point.

Finishing a Thread

To end a length of thread, bring the needle to the wrong side of the background fabric so that it is under the appliqué, just in from the edge. Take three stitches, slipping the thread through the loop of the last stitch to hold the thread securely. Clip the thread, and remove basting stitches after your appliqué is completed.

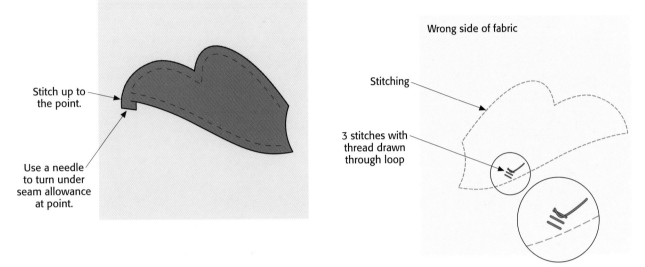

Stitch up to the point.

Use a needle to turn under seam allowance at point.

Wrong side of fabric

Stitching

3 stitches with thread drawn through loop

MACHINE APPLIQUÉ

The preparations for machine appliqué are the same as for hand appliqué. Baste your appliqué shapes with YLI Basting Thread. Be sure to baste finer areas like leaf points and notches carefully, because it will be too difficult to turn under the seam allowances when working in the needle area of the machine. Baste the appliqué shapes together to preconstruct the units needed for your project. Use high-quality supplies to make your machine appliqué more beautiful and easier to do.

Machine Needles

I recommend using a very fine machine needle, size 60/8, which has a short sewing life of about eight hours of stitching.

Thread

I use two types of thread. One is a clear nylon thread for the top of the machine that has a gauge size of .004. It is super fine and attaches an appliqué to background fabric invisibly. In the bobbin, I use a machine embroidery thread, size 30 or size 60/2. Match the bobbin thread color to the color of your background fabric.

Presser Foot

Attach the zigzag foot to your sewing machine. I recommend using a clear one, if possible, with a toe that has a center line. This type of foot makes it very easy to keep your appliqué centered as you stitch by machine because the toe holds the appliqué in place.

> TIP: Fill two bobbins with machine embroidery thread so that you won't run out of thread during a project. Mark the bobbins with a colored marker to indicate that they contain embroidery thread.

Machine Settings

Lower the top tension on your sewing machine until the bobbin thread no longer pulls to the surface when you stitch. Remember that you need to have enough tension to form stitches. When you have adjusted the tension correctly, write your tension settings down for future reference.

Increase the stitch length on your machine to approximately $\frac{3}{16}$" maximum length. Decrease the width of the zigzag stitch so that it barely catches the edge of your appliqué shapes. If you are appliquéing through layers of fabric and the bobbin thread appears, change the bobbin thread to a darker shade just for that area. If your machine has a slower sewing speed and automatic needle-down, these features will make stitching control easier.

> TIP: Practice machine appliquéing a few shapes to get the feel of your machine and to anticipate where to place the stitches. When pivoting around curves, leave the needle down in the fabric to keep the threads from pulling.

THE MIX-AND-MATCH OPTION

The appliqué patterns in this book are interchangeable; a leaf from one quilt will fit onto the flower from another. For example, you can exchange the leaf from the "Tulip and Thorn Leaf" quilt on page 28 with the leaf from the "Pomegranates" quilt on page 61. Or, you can replace the tulip with the flower from the "Spinner Flowers and Leaves" quilt on page 55. The wide assortment of pattern pieces in this book will enable you to create many interesting design combinations and create beautiful quilt designs of your own. The border sections from each of the quilts are also interchangeable. If you like the Nine Patch border from "Coverlet Tulips and Scrolls" and want to use it for "High Style," you can easily do this because the scale is the same. I have always enjoyed looking at appliqué patterns and finding ways to make changes and add my own personal touches, and I encourage you to do the same with the patterns in this book. You can get to the mix-and-match stage in just a few easy steps. All you need are a few basic supplies and a bit of time to allow the creative process to start flowing.

Selecting Fabrics

My students often say that they don't have enough imagination to know what a block will look like. My answer is that I don't always know what a block will look like, either, but that is part of the fun! Start by auditioning fabrics for your quilt. Cut scraps of any fabrics you'd like to use, and place them on a piece of your background fabric. View the fabrics through the wide end of a pair of binoculars and see if any fabric pops up at you like a discordant note. This simple process will help you decide if the colors you chose will work well in a finished quilt.

> TIP: Don't waste fabric at the designing stage—scraps are all you need to evaluate colors on background fabric.

Auditioning Appliqués

After you select the colors and fabrics you want to use in your quilt, move on to choosing the appliqué shapes you want to use in your design.

Making Photocopies

Start by making several photocopies of the pattern pieces for each appliqué shape you are thinking of using in your quilt. I like to make about half a dozen copies of each pattern piece. You can also trace individual shapes directly from the pages of this book, but this is more time-consuming. Cut out each pattern piece so that you can experiment with various layouts.

Choosing a Block Orientation

Decide on a block orientation for your 24" center block. The orientation of a block refers to the direction in which you will place the appliqué shapes. There are six basic block orientations featured in this book: outward, inward, U-shaped, spinning circle, basic wreath, and diamond (both square and on-point). Read through the following descriptions and let your personal preferences guide you in deciding which one you want for your quilt.

In the "Pomegranates" quilt block on page 61, the leaves are rooted under the corner brackets and the flowers point toward the center of the block. This is an example of an inward orientation. You could easily change this block to an outward orientation by making the pomegranate flowers face toward the corners, keeping the stems the same, and replacing the corner brackets with a center motif such as a circle. The "Fleur-de-Lys" quilt on page 77 has an outward block orientation, with the intersection of four stems covered by a symmetrical center motif and a center circle. You can close up a U-shape to create a wreath or vice versa. Look at the "Flowing Leaf" quilt on page 49 and think about how you could rearrange the leaves into a wreath entwined with the flowers.

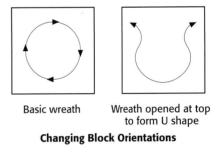

Basic wreath   Wreath opened at top
                      to form U shape

Changing Block Orientations

A spinning circle and a basic wreath both have a circular orientation, but a spinning circle will contain a design element coming outward from the circle, filling in the corner areas.

Basic wreath with appliqué pieces
that are used to fill in
empty corner areas;
becomes spinning circle

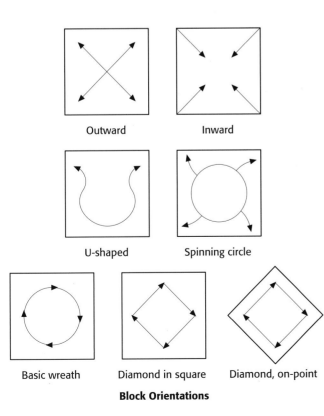

Outward   Inward

U-shaped   Spinning circle

Basic wreath   Diamond in square   Diamond, on-point

Block Orientations

In a diamond orientation, the design elements are placed on the diagonal, which can be very useful if you wish to enlarge a quilt by adding half-square triangles. In a diamond orientation, you can place the appliqués on-point while the block remains square, or place the appliqués straight and turn the block on-point and add half-square triangles. In the "Coverlet Tulips and Scrolls" quilt on page 82, for example, the center block could be placed on point within the quilt layout, and scrolls placed in half-square triangles.

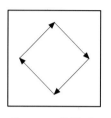
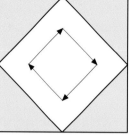

Square quilt block, with appliqué shapes arranged on-point

Quilt block on-point, with appliqué shapes set straight; half-square setting triangles form a square

Laying Out a Center Block

Cut a 24" square of blank white paper to represent a finished-size center block. Fold the paper square in half horizontally and vertically. Then fold it diagonally in both directions.

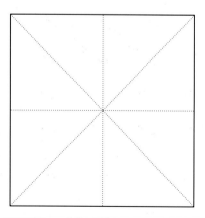

Crease 24" x 24" paper square horizontally, vertically, and diagonally.

Place your paper appliqué shapes on the 24" paper square in various configurations. Play and experiment with different arrangements, and enjoy coming up with different possibilities. When you have created an arrangement that pleases you, glue the paper appliqué shapes on the 24" paper square. With a pencil, do a little artwork to fill in stems or trace a circle here or there. This will give you an idea of the overall appearance of your design. Display your paper pattern in a prominent place for several days, and see how you feel about your design. This period of consideration is important because it allows you to take an objective look at your work. If you decide there is something about the design that doesn't please you, simply remove the photocopied appliqué shapes and try something else. When you decide on the layout you like, use a fine-tip, permanent black marker to do a clean line drawing of your center square. This will become your reference drawing and you can use it to prepare the templates for your design.

Negative Space

The term *negative space* refers to an area where there are no design elements. As you create quilt designs of your own, consider the concept of negative space. For example, the center block in "French Iris Wreath" on page 66 is just barely filled with appliqués, and the large areas of negative space give the design a quiet feeling. The blank corners are filled with quilting but a flower could just as easily be placed there.

If you want to place a center square on-point, think about how you would like to fill the half-square setting triangles that will surround it. The object is to fill in with appliqué and have a lavish quilt. In both the "Carnation and Acanthus Leaf" quilt on page 34, and the "Asters and Daisies" quilt on page 94, I have filled the large, dark half-square triangles with appliqués. I could just as easily have placed a large overall print in these areas and not added any more appliqué.

COMPLETING A QUILT

Border Treatments

Each of the projects in this book features a different type of border treatment. The pieced border sections are very easy to sew. Any special directions for a border are indicated in the project instructions. All seam allowances are ¼" except where noted in the project instructions.

> TIP: Cut the final (outside) borders for your quilt before cutting any strips needed for pieced borders.

Checkerboard and Nine Patch Borders

Checkerboard borders are easy to make with straight-grain strip sets. The checkerboard strip sets consist of strips in two different colors that are sewn together with a ¼" seam allowance, and the lighter fabric is pressed toward the darker fabric. The strip sets are rotary cut into the appropriate size segments for your project, flipped, and stitched into checkerboard sections.

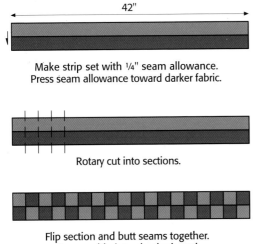

Make strip set with ¼" seam allowance.
Press seam allowance toward darker fabric.

Rotary cut into sections.

Flip section and butt seams together.
Reassemble into checkerboard.

Make Nine Patch borders with the same straight-grain strips you used for the checkerboard borders. Use three strips to form the strip sets as

shown below. Sew the seams with a ¼" seam allowance and press them in opposite directions to make it easier to align and sew the sections together accurately.

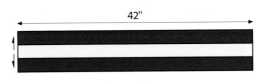

42"

Make 2 strip sets,
with darker fabric on top and bottom and lighter in center.
Press seam allowances toward darker fabric.

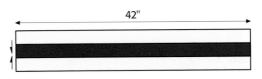

42"

Make 1 strip set,
with darker fabric in center.
Press seam allowances toward darker fabric.

Rotary cut 2 sections from first set and 1 from other set
to form nine-patch unit.

Make as many nine-patch units
as needed for your project.

Sawtooth Borders

To piece the Sawtooth units in the border of "Carnation and Acanthus Leaf" on page 34 and "French Iris Wreath" on page 66, use the bias strip-piecing technique. Cut an 18" x 18" square of each fabric. Layer the squares right sides together and cut them apart diagonally into the strip width you need. Sew the long bias edges together with a ¼" seam allowance, and press these seams open. Place the square template for the Sawtooth unit over the seam of the strip diagonally, and use a pencil for marking fabric to trace around the template. Rotary cut on your marked lines. You will need to make several of these strip units to make all of the Sawtooth units needed for a quilt. The number of bias square units needed is indicated in the project instructions.

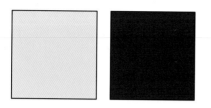

Cut 18" squares from selected fabrics.

Layer fabric with right sides together.

Rotary cut diagonally.

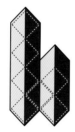

Combine 1 strip of each color to form bias strip.

Join multiple strips to form a unit. To avoid wasting fabric and to make Sawtooth units more quickly, make a template, trace around it, and rotary cut.

Dogtooth Borders

There are two types of Dogtooth borders in the projects in this book. The "Tulip and Thorn Leaf" quilt on page 28 has a two-triangle Dogtooth border, like the one shown at the top of the illustration. The "Asters and Daisies" quilt on page 94 features a one-triangle border with individual pieces added one at a time.

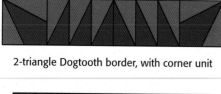

2-triangle Dogtooth border, with corner unit

1-triangle Dogtooth border, with corner unit

To make a two-triangle Dogtooth border, sew the two triangles together to form a rectangle unit, offsetting one triangle approximately ¼" at the top to ensure a proper fit. Join the correct number of units together to form a Dogtooth border in the length needed for your project.

Join 2 triangles to form a Dogtooth unit.

Join Dogtooth units to form border.

To make a one-triangle border, repeat the same process. Use the offset technique and add one triangle at a time. You can also chain stitch the pieces by sewing together two triangles at a time and then sewing the triangle units together. By doing this, you can form a larger section of the Dogtooth border quickly.

Add 1 triangle at a time to form a 1-triangle Dogtooth border.

Appliqué Borders

Several of the quilts feature appliqué borders, which are shown on the appliqué border diagram in the project instructions. Large-scale appliqué shapes fill a border area very quickly and require a border width of at least 6" to accommodate the placement of leaves and flowers. I developed the border for "Carnation and Acanthus Leaf" by playing with appliqué cutouts. It is not necessary to use all of the design elements present in a center block for an appliqué border; just a portion of a design often works well. For example, the border of the "Frilled Hearts" quilt on page 87 has a small flower in the heart center. A border of hearts would have been overpowering, but adapting a design from the center block adds variety. For scalloped borders, full-size border templates are provided.

Plain Borders

All of the quilts have plain outer borders. It is best to cut the outer border strips along the lengthwise grain of the fabric, which will not stretch. This helps avoid distortions along the outside edges of your quilt. Plain borders also help secure the edges of pieced borders.

Before attaching the outer borders to a quilt, measure the quilt top through the center in both directions to determine the length for the border strips. You may find that one or more of the sides of your quilt top will need to be eased onto the border strip in order to make the quilt turn out straight. If you need to ease more than ½", go back to your quilt top and either let out a few seams and restitch them, or take in a few seams. Take care to position the quilt top against the feed dogs while you attach the border strips so that the differential feed on your sewing machine will help ease in any fullness.

Mitering Border Corners

For several projects, it will be necessary to miter the border corners. A mitered corner has a 45° seam that joins two adjacent border strips. Begin by sewing the outer border strips to the sides of your quilt, starting and ending ¼" in from the edge of the quilt top. Backstitch to secure the beginning and end of each seam. Place your quilt top right side up on a large ironing surface and fold the border strips underneath themselves so that the folded edges meet and form a 45° angle. Place a protractor on the quilt top so that the 0° line lies exactly at the corner where the folded edges meet the corner of the quilt top. Make sure that the angle of the corner seam is accurate. Press a crease in the folded edges to establish the seam line, and place the right sides of the border strips together. Sew the corner seam from the corner of the quilt top outward. Trim the mitered seam allowance to ¼" and press it open. Repeat this process at each corner of the quilt top.

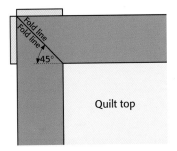

Pressing a Quilt Top

Lay a thick bath towel on a pressing surface and place your completed quilt top on top of the towel. Press the quilt top with a steam iron. Make sure that there are no twisted seams in the pieced border areas. Press appliquéd areas from the wrong side of the quilt top to raise the appliqué and to help eliminate ridges that can come from the seam allowances that are turned under.

> TIP: If your quilt top seems a bit limp from being handled during hand appliqué, spray the wrong side with sizing to restore its freshness.

Preparing the Backing

If your quilt is large and needs to have a seam in the backing, you can place the seam either at the middle or off to one side. Make sure that the backing will be a few inches wider and longer than your quilt top. Sew the seam with a ½" seam allowance and trim it to ¼" so that you can remove the selvages. Otherwise, these tightly woven edges will pucker and pull at the seam. Use thread that matches the backing fabric so that your stitches don't show. Press the backing seam open to avoid a thick ridge that is difficult to quilt through by hand. If you choose to use a side seam in your quilt backing, you will need one full width of fabric plus a section of a second width of fabric.

Quilting

When it comes to choosing quilting designs for a quilt, my motto is, "Keep it simple." The projects in this book feature mostly straight lines in backgrounds, outline quilting around appliqué shapes, and border quilting designs that reflect the style of the borders. Whatever type of quilting design you choose, it is important to distribute the amount of quilting evenly over the quilt surface. A center block filled in with stipple quilting and only a small amount of border quilting will become wavy at the edges and the center might bubble out. My guideline is to run my hand over the surface of a quilt. If there are puffy, unquilted areas, I know that more quilting is needed. You can accent certain areas within a quilt with more quilting. Variety adds interest in your quilt as well as dimension. For example, the center of the "Carnation and Acanthus Leaf" quilt on page 34 features a checkerboard pattern and the corners of the block are marked with lines following the shape of the corner. The scale of your quilt design should correspond to the scale of your quilting. If your border area is 6" wide, choose a design that fills in its width comfortably, as shown in the diagram. The same design in a smaller size could look sparse, as also shown in the diagram. Whichever way you decide to quilt your quilts, use the following guidelines for marking, choosing batting, layering and basting, and the tips for successful hand and machine quilting.

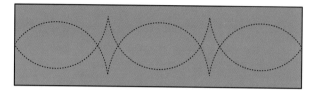

6" border with quilting design that is the correct size

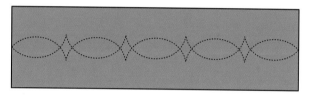

6" border with quilting design that is too small

Marking

When marking a quilt top, take your time and be careful so that the marked lines will not show after you finish quilting. If your background is a light fabric, place white paper underneath it to lighten the fabric and make it easier to mark. This will also help you keep your lines light. Use a light box underneath dark fabric to make your marked lines visible. I use either a silver pencil or a fine mechanical pencil for marking fabric. Test any marking tool you want to use on samples of the quilt fabric. When you test marking pencils on dark fabric, take a minute to turn off the light and see how dark your marked lines look. The goal is to mark lines only dark enough so that you can see them easily as you quilt.

Adequate light will keep you from marking your quilting lines too dark. If necessary, take a few days to mark a quilt top accurately and evenly. The end result will be worth the wait.

If you decide to use a purchased stencil, either measure the size of the stencil and make sure the identical measurements will fit the quilt top, or use banner paper and draw out the entire design you want to use. Banner paper, which measures 24" x 40' and comes on a roll, is available at many office supply stores. I prefer to draw out border sections so that there are no surprises during the marking process. Drawing a complete quilting design on paper will also help you see how a design will work at the corners of a quilt. If you need to make adjustments to make a motif fit or stretch a design to fill in a space, it's easy to do on paper before marking the quilt.

> TIP: Marked lines can fade over time or simply from handling a top as you quilt. If this happens, re-mark your lines just dark enough so that you can see the design again. It is better to re-mark lines than to remove lines that are too dark, which often leaves smudges, abraded spots, or causes you to launder a finished quilt immediately.

Choosing Batting

When it comes to choosing between polyester and cotton batting, think about how you want your quilt to look. Both types of batting have good characteristics. Cotton batting comes in a variety of thicknesses that produce varying amounts of loft, and cotton is well suited for machine quilting. Polyester batting, especially in a low-loft thickness, is very good for hand quilting. All of the projects in this book are intended for use as wall quilts, and either polyester or cotton batting will produce a lovely look. Once I choose my batting for a project, I usually cut it the same size as the quilt backing.

Layering and Basting

Baste the quilt top, batting, and backing fabric together with safety pins or basting thread. If you use thread, make your stitches long and place them in a grid of straight lines that are about 4" apart. If you like using safety pins, place them evenly all over the surface of the quilt "sandwich," and avoid pinning on your marked lines. Remember that safety pins will need to be removed as you reach them, whether you quilt by hand or machine. After layering and basting the quilt sandwich, check the backing fabric and smooth out any wrinkles.

Machine Quilting

Whether you use a walking foot to stitch straight filler lines or try free-motion quilting with a darning foot, you will find that two of the great advantages of machine quilting are that your stitch quality will always be consistent, and it's easy to do.

Free-motion quilting allows you to follow marked quilting lines or create free-form patterns such as zigzags, curves, or stippling with the use of a darning foot and lowered feed dogs on your sewing machine. You can move or guide the basted quilt layers freely underneath the foot of the sewing machine. Another type of free-motion quilting, outline quilting, involves quilting around the shapes in a block and moving the quilt rather than lifting the presser foot as you stitch. Free-motion quilting takes a bit of practice, but the center blocks for the projects in this book are a nice, manageable size, even if you are a beginner. To start a line of free-motion quilting, move the quilt very slowly so that you can take several tiny stitches in a row. Then begin moving the quilt more freely, guiding it underneath the needle in whatever type of free-motion pattern you select. Move the quilt smoothly, keeping the length of your stitches consistent. To end a line of free-motion quilting, move the quilt slowly again, taking several more tiny stitches in a row. You can either clip the threads close to the surface of the quilt or bury them in the batting layer as you would for hand quilting.

TIP: Have your sewing machine serviced before doing a lot of free-motion quilting. Insert a new needle before you start, and spray your worktable with silicone spray that has no additives so that you can slide a quilt around easily. On my plastic work surfaces, I use Slip and Slide by Dow Corning, which is available at hardware stores.

If you choose to stitch straight filler lines instead of free-form patterns, use a walking foot, raise the feed dogs, and if necessary, adjust the tension on your machine. To start a line of machine quilting when using a walking foot, adjust the stitch length on your machine and do a few very short stitches, move the setting to a regular stitch length again, and continue quilting. End a line of quilting with very short stitches, and clip the threads close to the surface of the quilt.

No matter what kind of machine quilting you choose, make sure to match the thread on top of your machine to the fabric in the area you want to quilt. Match the bobbin thread to your backing fabric. I use Mettler thread, size 50/3, for all of my machine quilting.

TIP: If you haven't had a lot of experience at machine quilting, make a practice quilt before you start quilting an actual quilt top. Layer a small square of fabric, batting, and backing. Try out the various settings on your machine, experiment with various threads, and practice using a walking foot and a darning foot. Once you determine which settings work the best, write them down for future reference.

Hand Quilting

Use either a hoop or a quilting frame for hand quilting. There are many different styles of both available. If you are using a hoop, you will need to baste the layers of your quilt together as described in "Layering and Basting" on page 24. There are some models of floor frames, however, that do not require basting the three layers together.

Next, determine the type of hand-quilting needle that will work best for your project. If you have not hand quilted in a while, I recommend using a size #9 Between needle, which is very sturdy and will still give you small stitches. As your hand quilting skill improves, try using a smaller needle, like a size #10 Between. Match the color of the quilting thread to the color of your backing fabric. Thread a needle with approximately an 18" length of thread and tie a knot in the end you cut. Make this knot large because you will want to hide it securely in the layers of the quilt sandwich. Pull the thread tight. Gently rub the knot into the top fabric. This gentle pressure will sink the knot into the quilt layers. Take a very small stitch to secure the knot in place.

To take the first stitch, hold the needle vertically so that it is perpendicular to the quilt top.

Insert it through the layers of the quilt sandwich and bring it back up again a short distance away. Using a rocking motion, fill your needle with a few stitches before you pull the thread all the way through the quilt sandwich. It is possible that you will need to practice quilting for several days to establish a rhythm. Keep working at it, and your stitches will become both small and even. Try to make your stitches as even on the back of the quilt as they are on the front. Check underneath the quilt from time to time to make sure that your stitches are even. To help your needle glide through the quilt layers, moisten a small cotton ball with silicone spray and rub the needle in the cotton ball to coat it with silicone. The silicone will not stain your fabric. As you quilt, respray the cotton ball and rub your needle with the silicone as needed.

Protect your finger on top of the quilt with a thimble, and the finger underneath the quilt as well. There are several products available that can be used for this purpose. A small disc with adhesive, another thimble, or a leather finger protector are among the many items that have worked well for quilters. The key is to experiment and find the method that is best for protecting your fingers.

To finish a line of hand-quilting stitches, bury a short length of thread inside the layer of batting. You can do this by tying a small knot at the end of the thread and pulling it into the batting or by backstitching through your line of quilting stitches. If you backstitch, make sure that your stitches do not look bulky. Clip the thread close to the surface of the quilt so that the tail end pulls back into the batting.

> TIP: Avoid quilting in the ditch because stitching in areas where there are thick seams will make for uneven stitches.

Binding Quilt Edges

The final step in completing a quilt is binding the edges. For all of the projects in this book, I have used single-layer bias binding. The width of the cut bias strips is 1½". Your bias binding will need to be as long as the four sides of your quilt, plus an extra 12" for the folded corners and overlapped ends of the binding. Cut as many bias strips as you need from fabric that is left after your project is finished. Using thread that matches your binding fabric and a ¼" seam allowance, sew the short ends of the bias strips together, as shown. Press the seam allowances open and trim the fabric tails even with the long sides of the binding. Or, if you prefer, press the seams to one side to eliminate the line of machine stitching that is visible when you press the seams open.

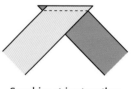

Sew bias strips together
with a ¼" seam allowance.

> TIP: Hand baste the raw edges of the quilt top together with ½" long stitches. Measure the sides of the quilt top, and the center, both horizontally and vertically. To ease-in uneven areas, tighten your basting stitches slightly. This works well for making adjustments up to ½".

To begin applying the binding to your quilt, leave a 6" length of the binding unstitched and folded up at a 45° angle. You can overlap this beginning length with the end of the binding later. Adjust the stitch length on your sewing machine to ten stitches per inch, and attach a walking foot. Using a ⅜" seam allowance, sew the binding to the raw edge of the quilt top. When you reach the first corner, stop stitching ⅜" in from the corner and backstitch to reinforce your stitching. Fold the binding up, creating a 45°-angle fold at the corner.

Fold the binding down so that it is even with the next side of the quilt top. Stitch the binding to this side of the quilt, starting ⅜" in from the edge of the quilt and taking a few backstitches. This line of stitching will start where your previous line of stitching ended. Repeat this process on all four sides of the quilt, and overlap or stitch the ends of the binding together, as desired.

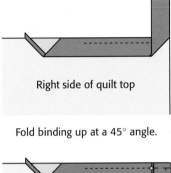

Fold binding up at a 45° angle.

Fold binding down again
and stitch to next side of quilt.

Fold the binding to the wrong side of the quilt and under itself. Stitch the folded edge of the binding to the backing fabric by hand. Use matching thread and be careful not to let your stitches come through to the front side of the quilt. Fold the corners on the back to create the mitered seams.

Fold the binding out at
45° angle at the corner.

Fold the next side of the binding in,
creating a 45° mitered corner seam.

Making a Label and Hanging Sleeve

The perfect finishing touch for your quilt is a label that includes your name, address, and information about the quilt itself. You should also attach a hanging sleeve. Make the sleeve at least 4" wide to accommodate the hanging rod and a bit shorter than the width of your finished quilt. Fold the short ends of the sleeve under and stitch a hem at each end. Align one long edge of the sleeve with the binding at the top edge of the quilt, and slipstitch the long edges of the sleeve in place on the backing.

TULIP AND THORN LEAF

TULIP AND THORN LEAF

by Sheila Wintle, 1999, Trenholm, Quebec, Canada, 56" x 56".
Circles and small leaves accent the extra-large tulips and
spiked thorn leaves in this colorful wall quilt.

CENTER BLOCK ORIENTATION: INWARD

Center Block Diagram

Materials

42"-wide fabric

¾ yd. medium green fabric for thorn leaves, stems, and vines

¾ yd. rust fabric for tulip centers, Dogtooth border, and appliqué border

½ yd. purple fabric for inner tulip petals and Dogtooth border

Fat quarter gold accent fabric for circles

Fat quarter dark green fabric for leaf liners

1¾ yds. multicolored print for outer tulip petals, final border, and binding

2½ yds. light background fabric for center block and appliqué border

3½ yds. fabric for backing

Batting of your choice, cut 3" larger than quilt top on all sides

Center Block

Cutting Chart

Fabrics	Pieces
Medium green	4 and 4 reversed thorn leaves
	4 bias strips for stems, each ⅞" x 5"
Rust	4 tulip centers
	4 small leaves
Purple	4 and 4 reversed inner tulip petals
Gold	5 circles
Dark green	4 and 4 reversed leaf liners
Multicolored	4 and 4 reversed outer tulip petals
Light background	25" x 25" center block

Appliqué Sequence

1. Prepare 4 bias stems as shown on page 13.

2. Referring to page 12, trace the appliqué pattern pieces on pages 32–33 onto template material and cut them out.

3. Referring to pages 12–13, trace the templates on the right side of the fabrics and cut out each appliqué.

4. Cut out the center block. Then press horizontal, vertical, and diagonal fold lines into the center block.

5. Following the numerical sequence indicated on the center block diagram, half-baste and preconstruct the tulip units. Make sure to clip the seam allowances of all pieces except for edges that will lie underneath other shapes. Refer to the center block diagram to determine where pieces overlap and clipping is not necessary.

   Note: *Turn under and baste only one point on the tulip centers because the inner tulip petals will cover the sides of these pieces. Leave the tips of the inner and outer tulip petals and leaves unbasted, and stitch these later with the needle-turn technique.*

6. Half-baste and preconstruct the thorn leaves and leaf liners in the same manner as for the tulip units.

7. Position and pin the stems, tulip units, and leaf units on the center block. Use the center block diagram as a placement guide. Place the stems on the pressed diagonal lines. Baste the appliqué units in place and remove the pins. Follow the perfect circle technique on pages 13–14 to prepare the circles. Baste them in place on the center block. Add the small leaves.

8. Appliqué the pieces and units to the center block.

   Note: *Leave the center seams of the thorn leaves open so that one side can be turned under and then cover the seam allowance of the other side.*

9. After appliquéing the pieces to the center block, press and trim the block to 24½" x 24½".

Dogtooth Border

Cutting Chart

Fabrics	Pieces
Rust	56 Dogtooth triangles
Purple	48 Dogtooth triangles
	4 Dogtooth corner triangles

Note: *In half of each border section, the piecing is reversed.*

Stitching Sequence

1. Sew together 4 Dogtooth border sections and 4 Dogtooth corner units as shown.

Make 4.

Make 4.

2. Measure the length of the border sections before adding them to the center block. Each pieced section should measure 24½"; if necessary, adjust the seam allowances in your piecing to ensure accuracy. Next, sew 2 of the pieced Dogtooth border sections to 2 sides of the center block. Sew a Dogtooth corner unit to each end of the remaining 2 Dogtooth sections, and sew these border sections to the remaining 2 sides of the quilt.

Appliqué Border

Cutting Chart

Fabrics	Pieces
Medium green	4 and 4 reversed thorn leaves
	4 bias strips for vines, each $\frac{7}{8}$" x 36"
Light background	Four $8\frac{1}{2}$" x 50" border strips on the lengthwise grain
Multicolored	4 and 4 reversed outer tulip petals
Purple	4 and 4 reversed inner tulip petals
Rust	4 tulip centers
	56 small leaves
Dark green	4 and 4 reversed leaf liners
Gold	48 circles

Appliqué Sequence

1. Prepare 4 bias vines as shown on page 13.
2. Sew the $8\frac{1}{2}$" x 50" border strips to the edges of the Dogtooth border. Miter the corner seams as shown on page 23.

3. Trace, cut out, half-baste, and preconstruct the tulip units and the thorn leaves with leaf liners as described in steps 2, 3, 5, and 6 of "Center Block." Prepare the circles with paper as before. Baste the sides of the small leaves, but leave the tips unbasted so that you can stitch them later with the needle-turn technique. Referring to the appliqué border diagram, position the appliqué units and pieces on the border. Remember to leave the seams of the leaf liners open. Pin the appliqué units and pieces to the border; baste them in place.

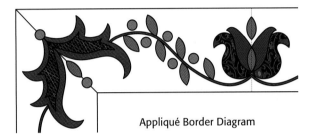

Appliqué Border Diagram

4. Remove the pins, and appliqué the pieces and units to the borders. Press your completed work.

Final Border

1. From the multicolored fabric, cut four $4\frac{1}{2}$" x 58" strips on the lengthwise grain.
2. Sew these border strips to the quilt top. Miter the corner seams.

Quilting and Finishing

1. Prepare the backing with a center seam. Trim the extra fabric from the sides so that the backing measures 60" x 60".
2. Layer and baste the backing, batting, and quilt top. Quilt as desired.
3. From the multicolored fabric, cut $1\frac{1}{2}$"-wide bias binding strips. You will need enough strips to go around the perimeter of the quilt plus 12" more for corners and overlap. Stitch the binding to the right side of the quilt top; then fold the binding to the back side of the quilt and slipstitch it in place, as shown on pages 26–27.

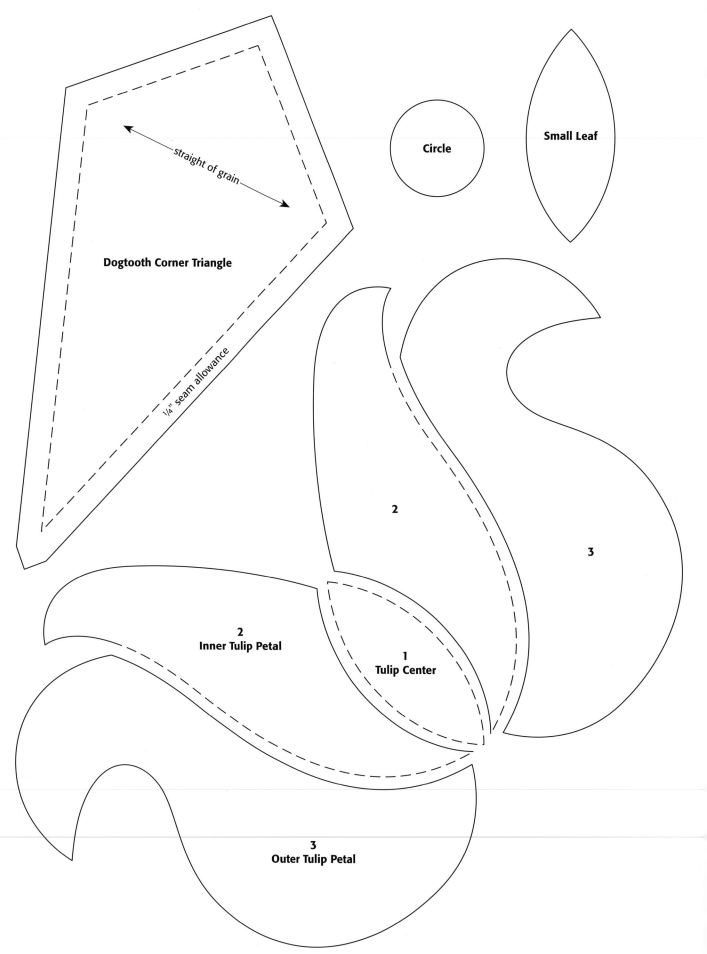

straight of grain

Dogtooth Corner Triangle

¼" seam allowance

Circle

Small Leaf

2

3

2
Inner Tulip Petal

1
Tulip Center

3
Outer Tulip Petal

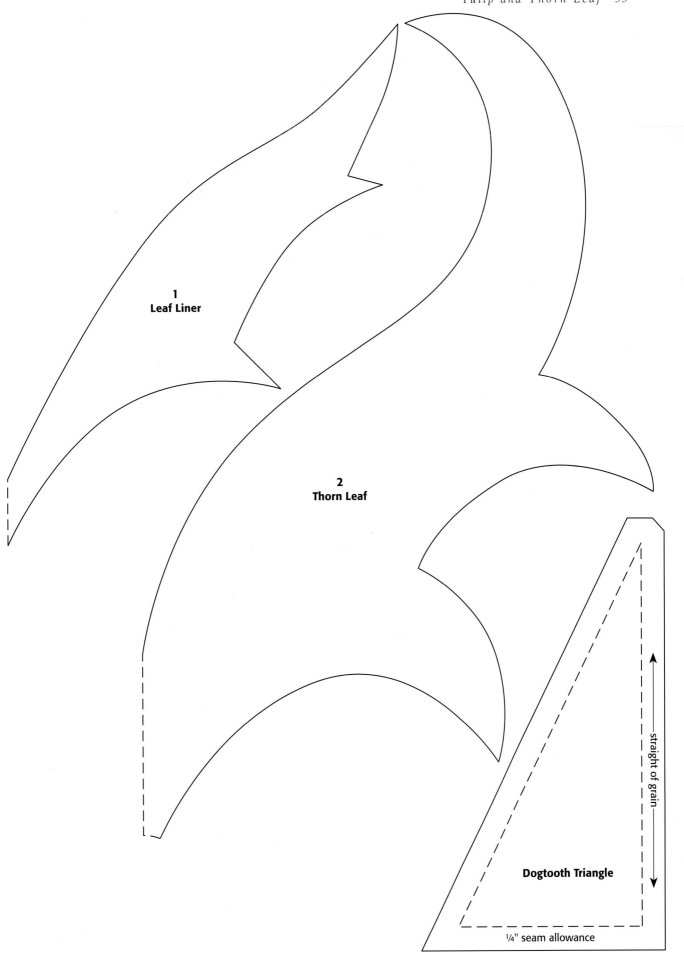

1
Leaf Liner

2
Thorn Leaf

straight of grain

Dogtooth Triangle

¼" seam allowance

CARNATION
AND ACANTHUS LEAF

CARNATION AND ACANTHUS LEAF

by Sheila Wintle, 1999, Trenholm, Quebec, Canada, 69½" x 69½".
A very high level of color contrast between the bright yellow and dark burgundy
gives this quilt lots of personality. It's a direct descendant of the colonial bed ruggs.

CENTER BLOCK ORIENTATION: BASIC WREATH, ON-POINT

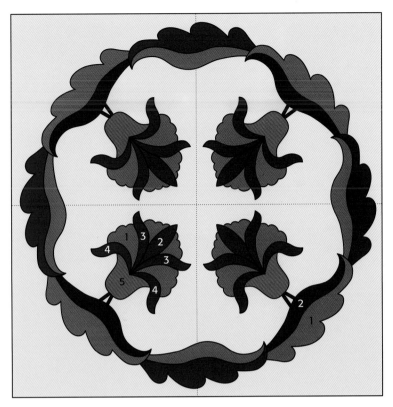

Center Block Diagram

Materials

42"-wide fabric

⅔ yd. dark green fabric for leaf tops, leaf bottoms, and stems

½ yd. each of 2 persimmon fabrics for flowers and leaves

4¼ yds. dark burgundy fabric for flowers, Sawtooth units, setting triangles, outer border, and binding

⅔ yd. light green fabric for leaf tops, leaf bottoms, and flower bases

4 yds. yellow fabric for background center block, Sawtooth units, and appliqué border

4 yds. fabric for backing

Batting of your choice, cut 3" larger than quilt top on all sides

Center Block

Cutting Chart

Fabrics	Pieces
Dark green	8 bias strips for stems, each ⅞" x 2"
	4 leaf tops
First persimmon	4 leaf tops
	4 flower backs
Second persimmon	4 leaf bottoms
Dark burgundy	4 leaf bottoms
	4 center petals
	4 and 4 reversed side petals
	4 and 4 reversed bottom petals
Light green	4 flower bases
Yellow	25" x 25" center block

Appliqué Sequence

1. Prepare the 8 bias stems as shown on page 13.
2. Referring to page 12, trace the appliqué pattern pieces on pages 39–40 onto template material and cut them out.
3. Referring to pages 12–13, trace the templates on the right side of the fabrics and cut out each appliqué.
4. Cut out the center block. Then press diagonal fold lines into the center block.
5. Following the numerical sequence indicated on the center block diagram, half-baste and preconstruct the flower units. Make sure to clip and baste only the upper edge of the flower back. Clip and baste the center, side, and bottom petals. Leave the tips open so that you can stitch them with the needle-turn technique later. Baste the petals to the flower backs; then add the flower bases. Position and pin the flower units on the diagonal folds of the center block, and place the stems underneath the flower bases. Measure the distance from the corner of the center block to the tip of the flower unit and make sure that all of the flowers reach this mark.
6. Half-baste and preconstruct the leaf units in the same manner described in step 5. Position and pin the basted leaf units in a circle around the flower units. Make sure that the tip of each leaf overlaps the end of the previous leaf.
7. Baste the appliqué pieces and units in place on the background fabric, remove the pins, and appliqué the pieces and units to the center block. After stitching the appliqués to the center block, press and trim the block to 24½" x 24½".

First Sawtooth Border

1. From the yellow and dark burgundy fabrics, cut 2 squares, each 18" x 18". Layer the fabrics right sides together. Using the template on page 40 and the Sawtooth bias strip-piecing method on pages 21–22, piece 48 Sawtooth units.
2. Sew 12 Sawtooth units together to make 1 Sawtooth border section. Make 4 Sawtooth border sections. Carefully place the light triangles in opposite directions in each half of these Sawtooth border sections. Sew 2 Sawtooth border sections to opposite sides of the center block as shown. From the yellow fabric, cut four 2½" squares. Sew one of these squares to each

end of the remaining 2 Sawtooth border sections and sew these Sawtooth border sections to the remaining sides of the center block, as shown.

Setting Triangles

Cutting Chart

Fabrics	Pieces
Dark burgundy	2 squares, each 20⅜" x 20⅜". Cut the squares diagonally in one direction to yield 4 half-square setting triangles.
Persimmon	4 flower backs
	4 flower bases
Light green	4 center petals
	4 and 4 reversed side petals
	4 and 4 reversed bottom petals
	2 and 2 reversed leaf tops
	2 and 2 reversed leaf bottoms
Dark green	2 and 2 reversed leaf tops
	2 and 2 reversed leaf bottoms

Stitching Sequence

1. Sew the setting triangles to the edges of the Sawtooth sections. Refer to the quilt photo on page 34 for placement guidance.
2. Trace, cut out, half-baste, and preconstruct 4 flower units and 8 leaf units as described in steps 2, 3, 5, and 6 of "Center Block." Position, pin, and baste the flower units and leaf units on the setting triangles. Note that there are 2 leaf units for each flower unit, and 1 of each pair of leaf units is reversed. Remove the pins and stitch the appliqués in place.

Second Sawtooth Border

1. From the dark burgundy and yellow fabrics, make 80 more Sawtooth units. Sew together 20 Sawtooth units to make 1 Sawtooth border section. Make 4 border sections. Take care to place the Sawtooth units in one direction in half of each section, and in the opposite direction in the other half.
2. Sew 2 Sawtooth border sections to opposite sides of the quilt top. From the dark burgundy fabric, cut four 2½" squares for the corners. Sew a square to each end of the remaining 2 Sawtooth border sections, and sew these border sections to the remaining 2 edges of the quilt top.

Appliqué Border

Cutting Chart

Fabrics	Pieces
Yellow	2 strips, each 7½" x 43"
	2 strips, each 7½" x 57"
First and second persimmons	8 flower backs
	4 and 4 reversed leaf bottoms
Light green	8 and 4 reversed leaf bottoms
	6 and 6 reversed leaf tops
	8 flower bases
Dark green	4 leaf bottoms
	6 and 6 reversed leaf tops
Dark burgundy	8 center petals
	8 and 8 reversed side petals
	8 and 8 reversed bottom petals

Appliqué Sequence

1. Sew the two 7½" x 43" strips to the top and bottom edges of the quilt. Trim them slightly to fit, if necessary.
2. Sew the two 7½" x 57" strips to the sides of the quilt top. Trim them slightly to fit, if necessary.
3. Trace, cut out, half-baste, and preconstruct 4 flower units and 8 leaf units as described in steps 2, 3, 5 and 6 of "Center Block." Note that there are 2 leaf units for each flower unit, and 1 of each pair of leaf units is reversed. Position, pin, baste, and appliqué them diagonally to the corners of the border. Refer to the quilt photo on page 34 for placement guidance.

4. For the centers of the borders, trace, cut out, half-baste, and preconstruct 4 flower units and 8 double leaf units. Refer to the quilt photo on page 34 for color and placement guidance. Rather than following an appliqué border diagram for placing the appliqués, position the flower units at the center of each side of the border. Arrange the leaves so that they come out on either side. Stitch the appliqués in place.

Final Sawtooth Border

1. For the final Sawtooth border, make 116 more Sawtooth units from the burgundy and yellow fabrics.
2. From the dark burgundy fabric, cut four 2½" squares for the border corners.
3. Sew 29 Sawtooth units together to make 1 Sawtooth border section. Be sure to place all of the Sawtooth units in the same direction as shown. This will produce an odd corner arrangement, but the symmetry is maintained because all corners will have this configuration.
4. Sew the dark burgundy squares to the ends of 2 Sawtooth border sections.
5. Sew the 2 border sections without the dark burgundy squares to opposite sides of the quilt. Sew the remaining 2 Sawtooth border sections with the dark burgundy squares to the remaining 2 sides of the quilt.

Final Border

1. From the burgundy fabric, cut two 4½" x 62½" strips. Sew these strips to the top and bottom edges of the quilt. Trim the strips slightly to fit, if necessary.
2. From the burgundy fabric, cut 2 more strips, each 4½" x 70½". Sew these strips to the sides of the quilt. Trim the strips slightly to fit, if necessary.

Quilting and Finishing

1. Prepare the backing with a center seam and trim the extra fabric from the sides so that the backing measures 74" x 74".
2. Layer and baste the backing, batting, and quilt top. Quilt as desired.
3. From the dark burgundy fabric, cut 1½"-wide bias binding strips. You will need enough strips to go around the perimeter of the quilt plus 12" more for corners and overlap. Stitch the binding to the right side of the quilt top; then fold the binding to the back side of the quilt and slipstitch it in place, as shown on pages 26–27.

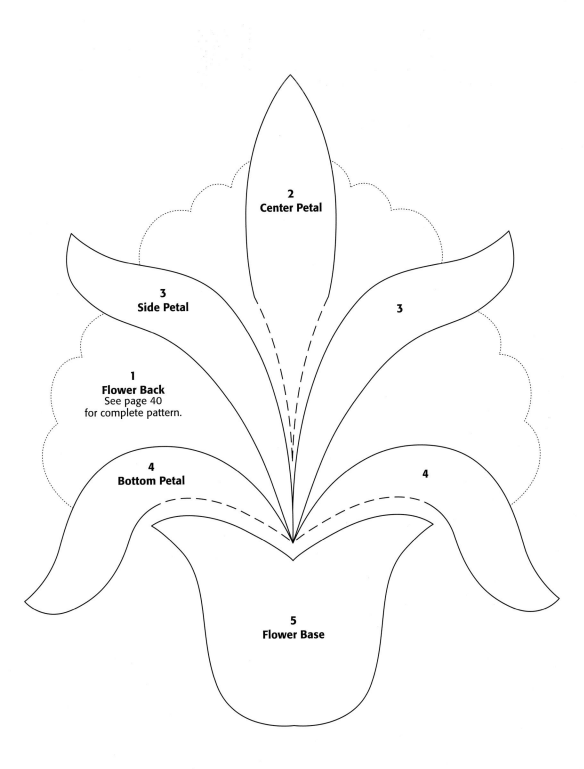

2
Center Petal

3
Side Petal

3

1
Flower Back
See page 40
for complete pattern.

4
Bottom Petal

4

5
Flower Base

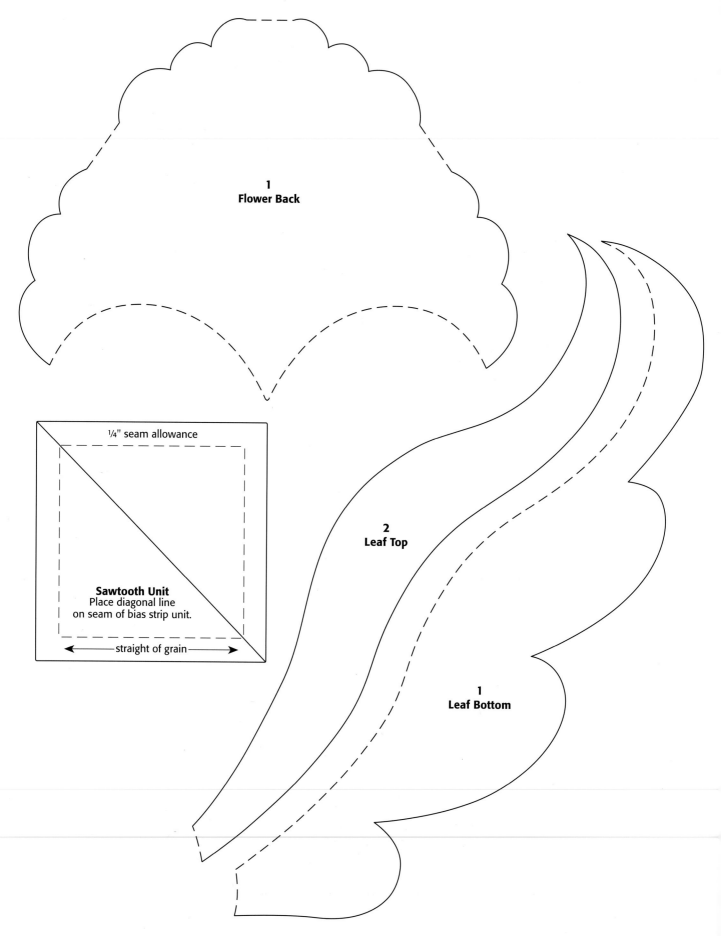

1
Flower Back

¼" seam allowance

Sawtooth Unit
Place diagonal line
on seam of bias strip unit.

← straight of grain →

2
Leaf Top

1
Leaf Bottom

ROSE RING

ROSE RING
by Sheila Wintle, 1999, Trenholm, Quebec, Canada, 44" x 44".
A bed rugg from Colonial Williamsburg in Virginia inspired me to create "Rose Ring."
I scaled down the size of the roses to make them more manageable for appliqué.

CENTER BLOCK ORIENTATION: WREATH

Center Block Diagram

Materials

42"-wide fabric

Fat quarter of gold fabric for rose center inserts and ring
Fat quarter of pink fabric for rose centers, outer leaves, and small leaves
2 yds. multicolored fabric for roses, small leaves, inner and outer scalloped sections, and binding
Fat quarter of green fabric for outer and small leaves
Fat quarter of blue fabric for leaf liners, small leaves, and large leaves
2 yds. light background fabric for center block and appliqué border
2⅔ yds. of fabric for backing
Batting of your choice, cut 3" larger than quilt top on all sides

Center Block

Cutting Chart

Fabrics	Pieces
Gold	4 rose center inserts
	6 bias strips, each ⅞" x 5½"
Pink	4 rose center circles
	2 outer leaves
Multicolored	4 complete sets of rose petals
	8 small leaves
Green	4 outer leaves
	6 small leaves
Blue	2 large leaves
	14 small leaves
Light background	25" x 25" center block

Appliqué Sequence

1. Prepare the 6 bias strips as shown on page 13.
2. Referring to page 12, trace the appliqué pattern pieces on pages 44–45 onto template material and cut them out.
3. Referring to pages 12–13, trace the templates on the right side of the fabrics and cut out each appliqué.
4. Cut out the center block. Then press horizontal, vertical, and diagonal fold lines into the center block.
5. Following the numerical sequence indicated on the center block diagram, half-baste and preconstruct 4 rose units.

   Note: *On the rose petals, clip only the sides that need to be basted.*
6. Half-baste and preconstruct 4 green outer leaf units with small blue leaves in the same manner as step 5.
7. Half-baste and preconstruct the 2 pink leaf units that are centered on the gold ring.

   Note: *One of the multicolored small leaves will need to be placed underneath a pink outer leaf for each of the units.*
8. Position, pin, and baste the bias strips to the center block. Refer to the center block diagram for placement of the strips. It is best to use individual pieces of bias strips for the gold ring to avoid thickness underneath the rose and leaf units. Trim any excess length from each bias strip after you position the rose units over them.

> TIP: Vary the color of your rose petals. A few fat quarters of colors you like are all you need to create a new color scheme. Work with a range of dark to light shades of a color. Make each petal a different shade. Use the texture provided by a print to add dimension to the rose.

9. Position, pin, and baste the rose units, leaf units, and small leaves in place on the center block. Use the center block diagram as a placement guide. Remove the pins and appliqué the units and pieces to the center block; then press and trim the block to 24½" x 24½".

Appliqué Border

Cutting Chart

Fabrics	Pieces
Multicolored	4 inner scalloped sections 4 outer scalloped sections
Light background	4 strips, each 10½" x 46", on the lengthwise grain
Pink	8 small leaves
Green	4 small leaves

Appliqué Sequence

1. Trace the scalloped border appliqué pattern pieces on pages 46–48 onto template material and cut them out.
2. Trace the templates on the right side of the fabric and cut out each inner and outer scalloped border appliqué.
3. Press a crosswise center fold in each of the 10½" x 46" strips. These fold lines will act as reference points for placing the scalloped sections. Clip and baste the edges of the scalloped sections before you appliqué them. Baste the inner and outer scalloped sections on either edge of these strips, matching the centers. Appliqué the scalloped edges in place, leaving the angled edges open below the **X** marks so that you can miter the corner seams later. If your appliqué is very secure, you can trim away the excess background fabric underneath the inner and outer scalloped sections to eliminate extra thickness and make hand quilting easier.

> TIP: Press the basted edges of the inner and outer scalloped sections for smooth, easy-to-stitch curves.

4. Sew the appliqué border to the sides of the center block so that the inner scalloped sections lie next to the center block. Start and stop each line of stitching ¼" in from the edge of the center block, and miter the corner seams, as shown on page 23.

5. Trace, cut out, and appliqué 3 small leaves at the corners of the appliqué border. Use the same template from "Center Block." Place 1 leaf on the diagonal seam and 2 leaves on either side. Refer to the photo on page 41 for placement guidance.

Quilting and Finishing

1. Prepare the backing with a center seam. Trim the extra fabric from the sides so that the backing measures 48" x 48".

2. Layer and baste the backing, batting, and quilt top. Quilt as desired.

3. From the multicolored fabric, cut 1½"-wide bias binding strips. You will need enough strips to go around the perimeter of the quilt plus 12" more for corners and overlap. Stitch the binding to the right side of the quilt top; then fold the binding to the back side of the quilt and slipstitch it in place, as shown on pages 26–27.

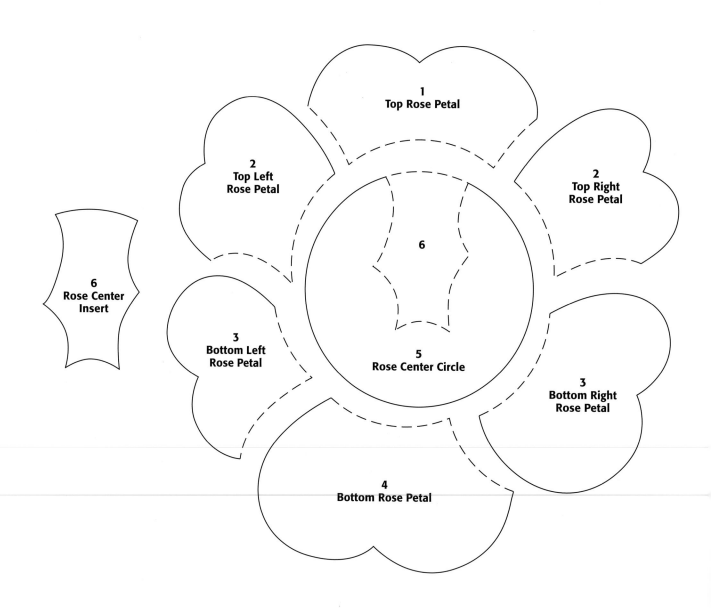

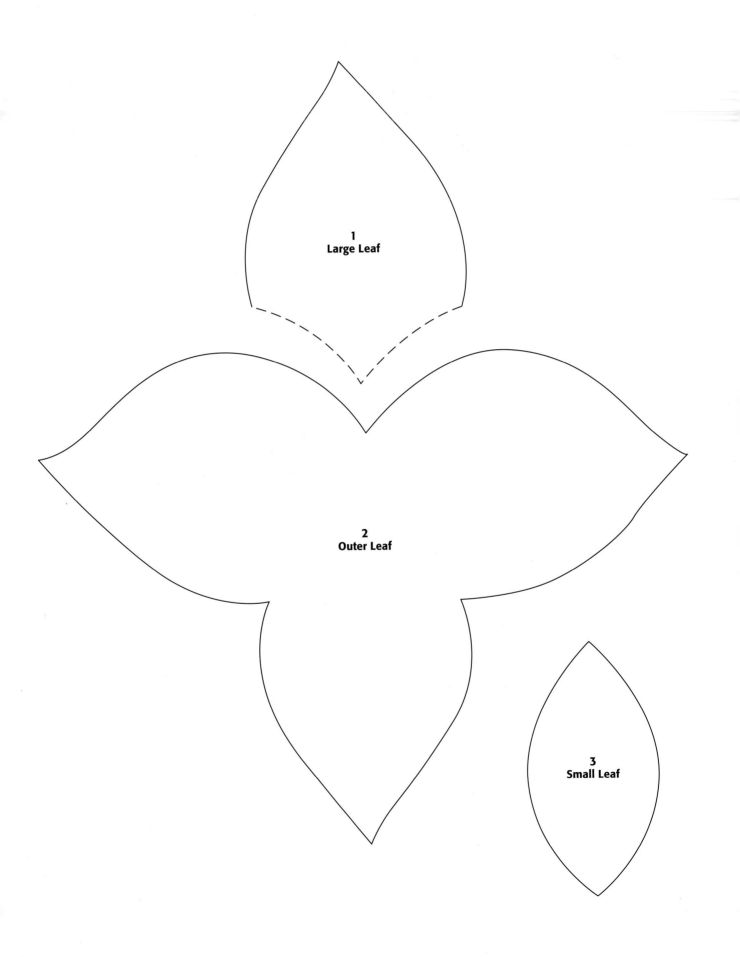

1
Large Leaf

2
Outer Leaf

3
Small Leaf

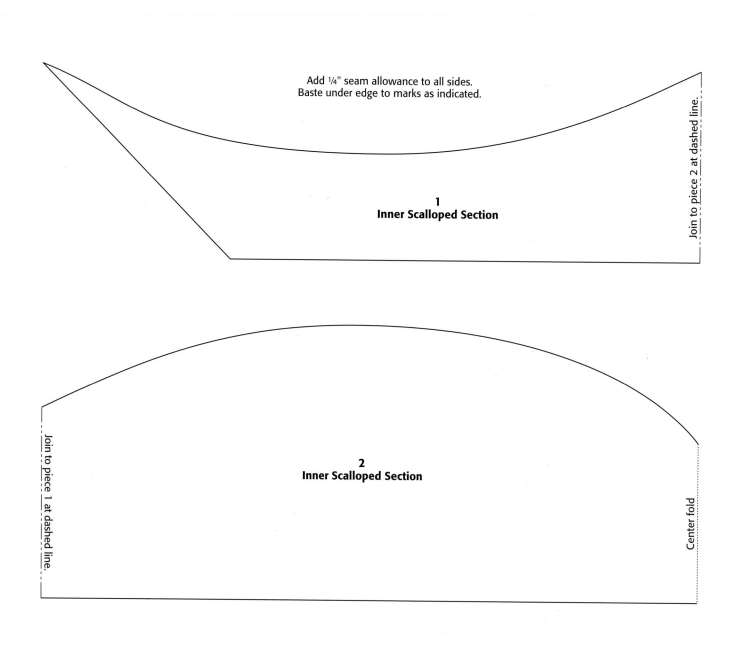

Add ¼" seam allowance to all sides.
Baste under edge to marks as indicated.

1
Inner Scalloped Section

Join to piece 2 at dashed line.

2
Inner Scalloped Section

Join to piece 1 at dashed line.

Center fold

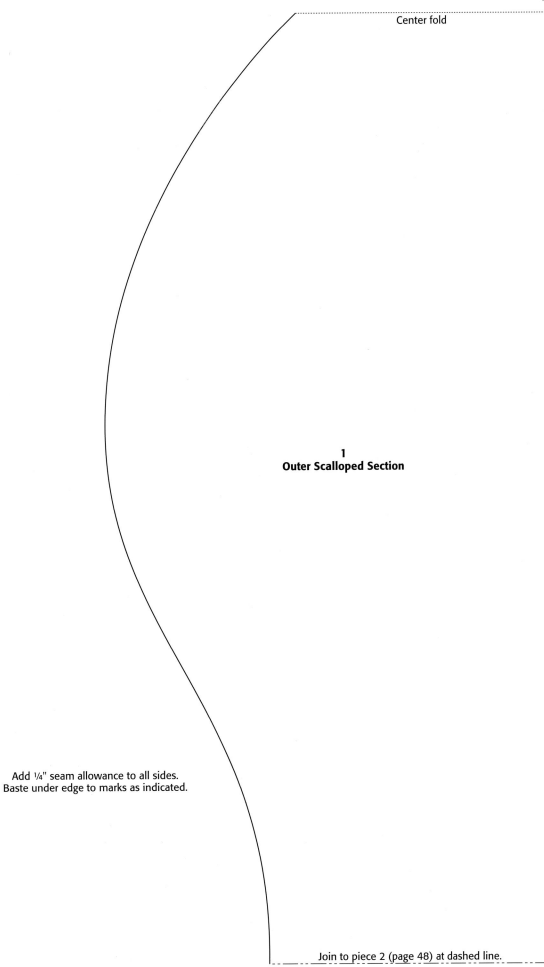

Center fold

1
Outer Scalloped Section

Add ¼" seam allowance to all sides.
Baste under edge to marks as indicated.

Join to piece 2 (page 48) at dashed line.

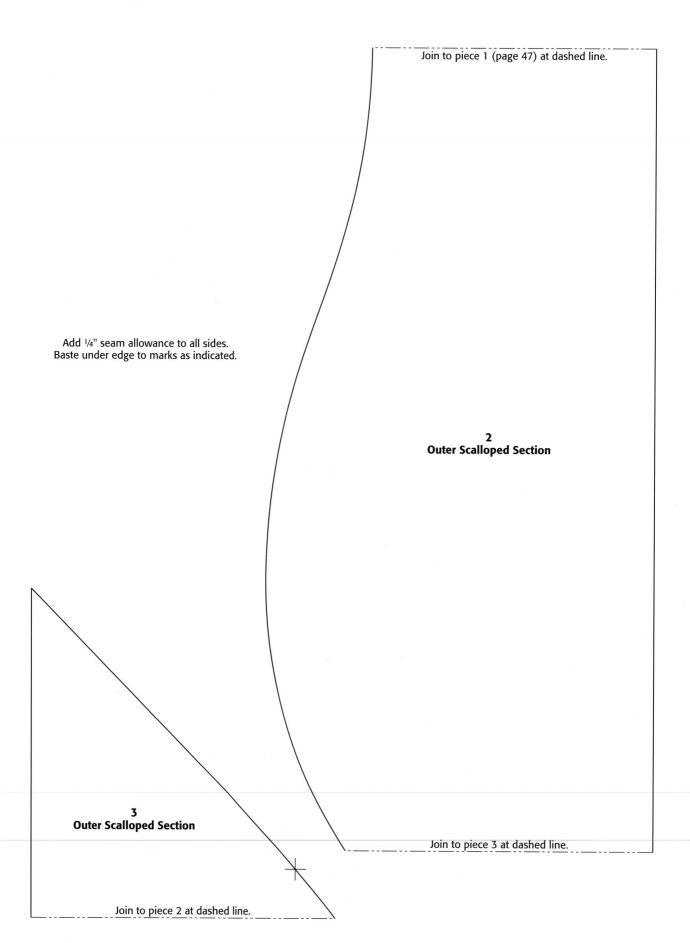

Join to piece 1 (page 47) at dashed line.

Add ¼" seam allowance to all sides.
Baste under edge to marks as indicated.

2
Outer Scalloped Section

3
Outer Scalloped Section

Join to piece 3 at dashed line.

Join to piece 2 at dashed line.

FLOWING LEAF

FLOWING LEAF

by Sheila Wintle, 1999, Trenholm, Quebec, Canada, 40" x 40".
The abstract flowers and bright colors in this quilt give it a more contemporary
feel than the look of the traditional colonial bed ruggs.

CENTER BLOCK ORIENTATION: U-SHAPED

Center Block Diagram

Materials

42"-wide fabric

Fat quarter of medium green fabric for stems
¾ yd. dark multicolored fabric for flowing leaves, base leaves, circles, and appliqué border
⅔ yd. dark fuchsia fabric for main flowers, circles, final border, and binding
Fat quarter of orange fabric for main flowers and circles
Fat quarter of teal fabric for bottom flower and circles
Fat quarter of bright blue fabric for outer points and circles
1¾ yds. light background fabric for center block and appliqué border
2½ yds. of fabric for backing
Batting of your choice, cut 3" larger than quilt top on all sides

Center Block

Cutting Chart

Fabrics	Pieces
Medium green	2 bias strips, each ⅞" x 5"
	4 bias strips, each ⅞" x 6"
Dark multicolored	2 and 2 reversed flowing leaves
	1 and 1 reversed base leaf
	3 circles
Dark fuchsia	2 main flowers
	1 outer scalloped center for bottom flower
Orange	2 main flowers
	1 circle

Teal	1 inner scalloped center for bottom flower
	2 circles
Bright blue	2 and 3 reversed outer points for bottom flower
	2 circles
Light background	25" x 25" center block

Appliqué Sequence

1. Prepare the 6 bias stems as shown on page 13.
2. Referring to page 12, trace the appliqué pattern pieces on pages 52–53 onto template material and cut them out.
3. Referring to pages 12–13, trace the templates on the right side of the fabrics and cut out each appliqué.
4. Cut out the center block. Then press horizontal and vertical fold lines into the center block.
5. Following the numerical sequence indicated on the center block diagram, half-baste and preconstruct the bottom flower unit. The remaining appliqué pieces only need to be clipped and basted individually.
6. Position and pin the stems, main flowers, flowing leaves, bottom flower, and base leaves on the center block. Use the center block diagram as a placement guide. Prepare the circles with the perfect circle technique described on pages 13–14. Baste all of the appliqués in place and remove the pins.
7. Appliqué the units and pieces to the center block; then press and trim the block to 24½" x 24½".

Appliqué Border

Cutting Chart

Fabrics	Pieces
Multicolored	4 scalloped sections
	4 finial corner points
Light background	4 strips, each 6½" x 36½"
Orange	3 circles
Teal	3 circles
Bright blue	3 circles
Dark fuchsia	3 circles

Appliqué Sequence

1. Trace the scalloped border appliqué pattern pieces and finial corner points on page 54 onto template material and cut them out.
2. Trace the templates on the right side of the fabric and cut out each appliqué.
3. Cut out the light background strips. Then press a crosswise center fold in each 6½" x 36½" strip. These fold lines will act as reference points for placing the scalloped sections.
4. Clip and baste under the raw edge of only the top edge of each scalloped section. Leave the angled ends and the straight, long, raw edges unbasted. Press the basted scalloped edges for smooth, crisp folds and easier stitching. Lay a scalloped section on a background strip, matching the centers. Baste the scalloped section in place and appliqué it to the background strip. Leave the ends unstitched so that you can miter the corner seams later. Repeat for the remaining scalloped sections and background strips.
5. Sew the appliqué border strips to the center block so that the scalloped shapes lie next to the center block. The scalloped curves should face the outer edge of the quilt. Start and stop each line of stitching ¼" in from the edge of the center block. Miter the corner seams as shown on page 23.
6. Baste the 4 finial corner points. Leave the blunt tips unbasted and place them over the raw edges at the ends of the scalloped sections. The accent circles will cover the tips. Baste the finial corner

points in place and stitch them to the appliqué border.

7. Prepare the circles with the perfect circle technique on pages 13–14. Spray the basted circles with spray sizing and press them to retain their circular shapes. Remove the paper circles and stitch the circles to the appliqué border. Refer to the quilt photo on page 49 for placement guidance.

Final Border

1. From the dark fuchsia fabric, cut 4 strips, each 2½" x 41" on the crosswise grain.
2. Sew the border strips to the sides of the quilt. Start and stop the stitching lines ¼" in from the edge of the quit top. Miter the corner seams as shown on page 23.

Quilting and Finishing

1. Prepare the backing with a center seam. Trim the extra fabric from the sides so that the backing measures 44" x 44".
2. Layer and baste the backing, batting, and quilt top. Quilt as desired.
3. From the dark fuchsia fabric, cut 1½"-wide bias binding strips. You will need enough strips to go around the perimeter of the quilt plus 12" more for corners and overlap. Stitch the binding to the right side of the quilt top; then fold the binding to the back side of the quilt and slipstitch it in place, as shown on pages 26–27.

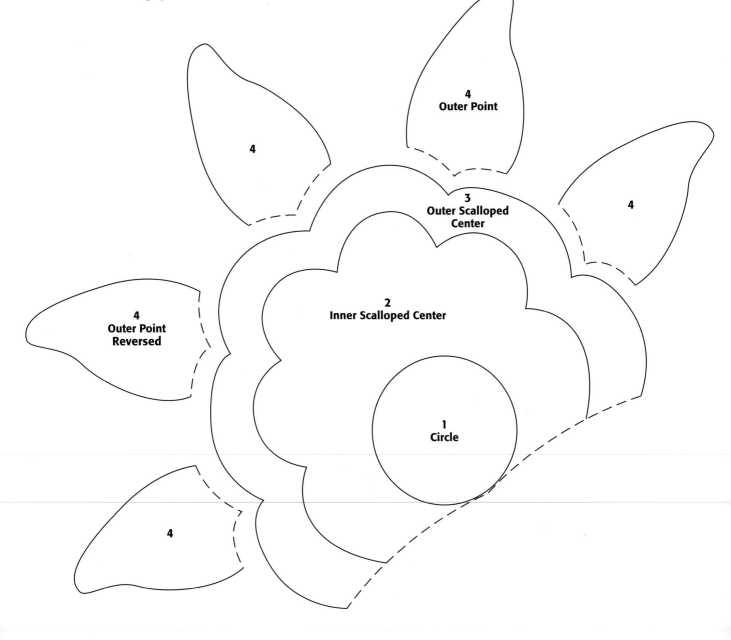

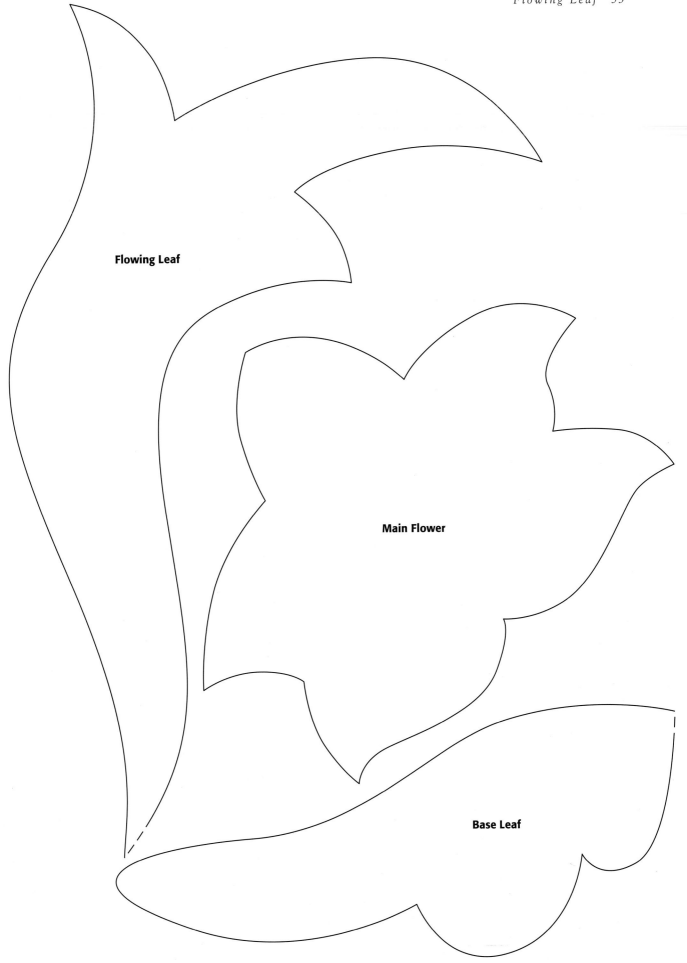

Flowing Leaf

Main Flower

Base Leaf

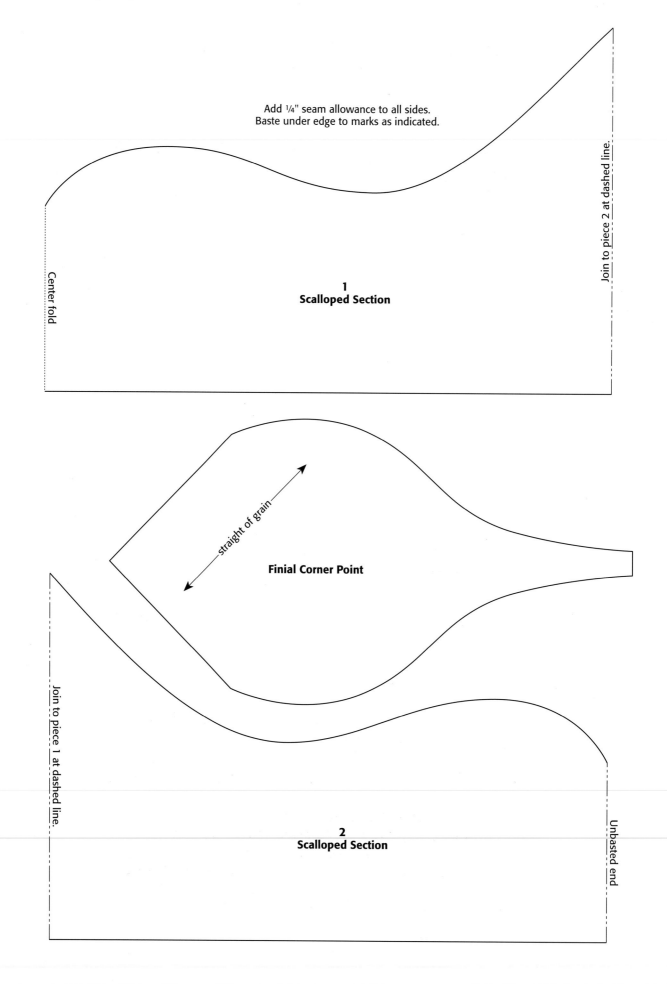

Add ¼" seam allowance to all sides.
Baste under edge to marks as indicated.

1
Scalloped Section

Center fold

Join to piece 2 at dashed line.

straight of grain

Finial Corner Point

Join to piece 1 at dashed line.

2
Scalloped Section

Unbasted end

SPINNER FLOWERS
AND LEAVES

SPINNER FLOWERS AND LEAVES
by Sheila Wintle, 1999, Trenholm, Quebec, Canada, 40" x 40".
This quilt design was inspired by smaller secondary designs often featured
on colonial bed ruggs. I made the elements larger to make it easier to appliqué them.

CENTER BLOCK ORIENTATION: OUTWARD

Center Block Diagram

Materials

42"-wide fabric

Fat quarter of light green fabric for stems, leaf tops, and spinner leaves

1 yd. bright pink fabric for flower tops and outer borders

Fat quarter of medium pink fabric for flower petals

Fat quarter of dark pink fabric for flower centers and circles

½ yd. medium green fabric for leaf centers and inner border

½ yd. dark green fabric for leaf bottoms, spinner leaves, and binding

1 yd. light background fabric for center block, outer border corners, and half-square triangles

2½ yds. of fabric for backing

Batting of your choice, cut 3" larger than quilt top on all sides

Center Block

Cutting Chart

Fabrics	Pieces
Light green	4 bias strips, each ⅞" x 8½"
	4 and 4 reversed leaf tops
	2 spinner leaves
Bright pink	4 flower tops
Medium pink	4 and 4 reversed flower petals
Dark pink	4 flower centers
	1 circle
Medium green	4 and 4 reversed leaf centers
Dark green	4 and 4 reversed leaf bottoms
	2 spinner leaves
Light background	25" x 25" center block

Appliqué Sequence

1. Prepare 4 bias stems as shown on page 13.
2. Referring to page 12, trace the appliqué pattern pieces on pages 59–60 onto template material and cut them out.
3. Referring to pages 12–13, trace the templates on the right side of the fabrics and cut out each appliqué.
4. Cut out the center block. Then press horizontal, vertical, and diagonal fold lines into the center block.
5. Following the numerical sequence indicated on the center block diagram, half-baste and preconstruct 4 flower and 8 leaf units. Make sure to clip the seam allowances of all pieces except for edges that will lie underneath other shapes. Refer to the center block diagram to determine where pieces overlap and clipping is not necessary.
6. Baste the stems in place on the center block. Use the diagonally pressed folds as placement guides. Allow ¼" seam allowances at each end to be tucked under the flower units and spinner leaves. Position, pin, and baste the flower and leaf units to the center block. Use the center block diagram as a placement guide.
7. Remove the pins and appliqué the center block. Appliqué the spinner leaves and center circle after the stems are in place. After stitching the center block, press and trim the block to 24½" x 24½".

Inner Border

- -

Cutting Chart

Fabrics	Pieces
Medium green	4 strips, each 2½" x 24½"
Medium pink	4 squares, each 2½" x 2½"

Stitching Sequence

1. Sew 2 medium green strips to opposite sides of the center block
2. Sew a medium pink square to each end of the 2 remaining medium green strips. Sew these strips to the remaining 2 sides of the center block.

Outer Border

- -

Cutting Chart

Fabrics	Pieces
Bright pink	4 strips, each 6½" x 28½" 2 flower tops
Light background	2 squares, each 6½" x 6½" One 12⅜" x 12⅜" square
Light green	2 and 2 reversed leaf tops 4 spinner leaves
Dark green	2 and 2 reversed leaf bottoms 4 spinner leaves
Dark pink	2 flower centers 4 circles
Medium pink	2 and 2 reversed flower petals
Medium green	2 and 2 reversed leaf centers

Stitching Sequence

1. Cut one end of 2 of the bright pink border strips at a 45° angle that goes from left to right. Cut the remaining 2 bright pink border strips in the same manner but with the 45° angle facing from right to left, as shown

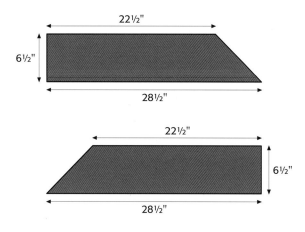

2. Cut the 12⅜" x 12⅜" background square diagonally into 2 half-square triangles.

3. Sew the 2 bright pink border strips with the 45° angles facing from left to right to the top and bottom edges of the first border, as shown. Then sew the 6½" background squares to the straight edges of the 2 bright pink border strips with the 45° angles facing from right to left, as shown. Sew these pieced border strips to the remaining 2 edges of the first border. Sew the 2 background half-square triangles to the remaining 2 corners of the quilt, as shown.

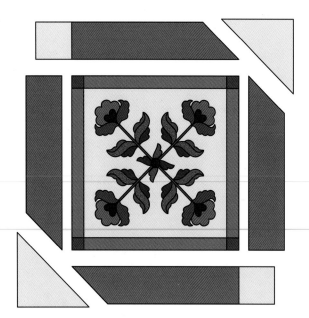

4. Trace, cut out, and appliqué 4 spinner leaves and a circle in the corner squares. Refer to the quilt photo on page 55 for placement guidance. Prepare the circles with the perfect circle technique shown on pages 13–14.

5. For each half-square triangle corner, trace, cut out, half-baste, and preconstruct 2 flower units and 4 leaf units as described in steps 2, 3, and 5 of "Center Block." Stitch the appliqués in place, adding between the leaf units a circle that has been made using the perfect circle technique.

Quilting and Finishing

1. Prepare the backing with a center seam. Trim the extra fabric from the sides so that the backing measures 44" x 44".

2. Layer and baste the backing, batting, and quilt top. Quilt as desired.

3. From the dark green fabric, cut 1½"-wide bias binding strips. You will need enough strips to go around the perimeter of the quilt plus 12" more for corners and overlap. Stitch the binding to the right side of the quilt top; then fold the binding to the back side of the quilt and slipstitch it in place, as shown on pages 26–27.

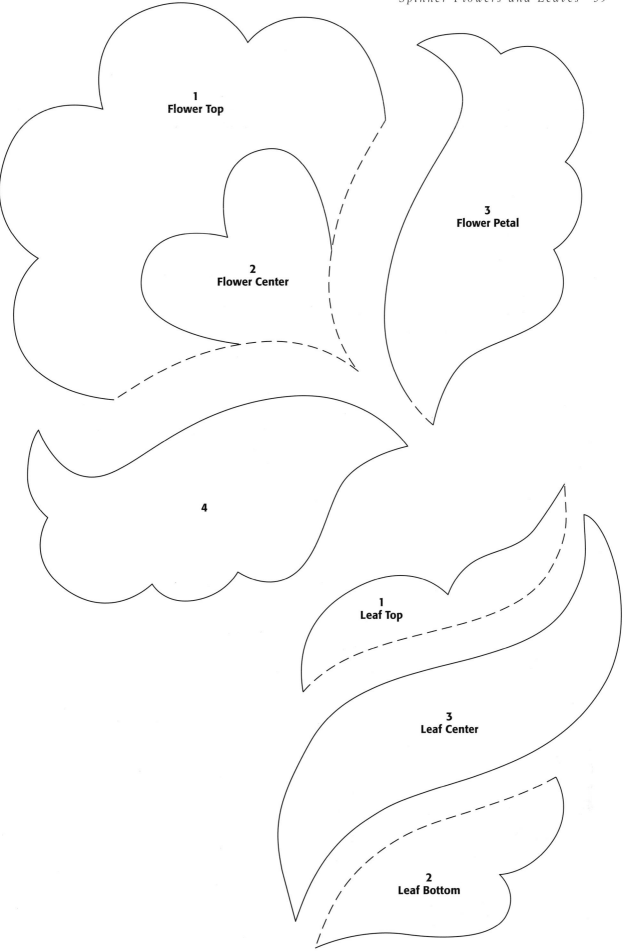

1
Flower Top

2
Flower Center

3
Flower Petal

4

1
Leaf Top

3
Leaf Center

2
Leaf Bottom

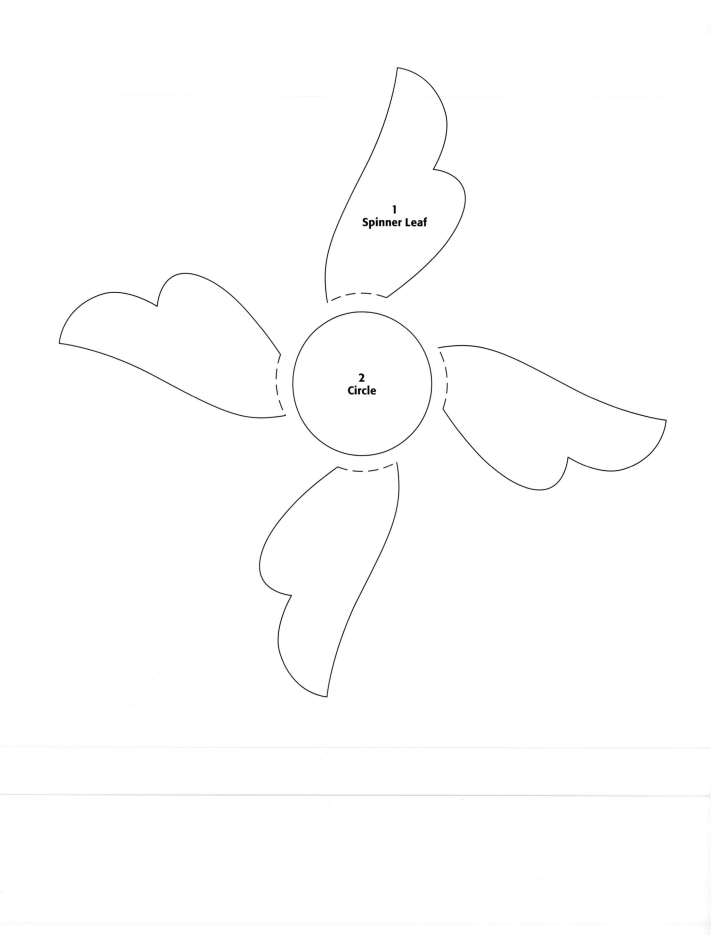

POMEGRANATES

POMEGRANATES

by Sheila Wintle, 1999, Trenholm, Quebec, Canada, 40" x 40".
This lovely flower was very popular in bed rugg designs.
My quilt contains a simplified version of the design.

CENTER BLOCK ORIENTATION: INWARD

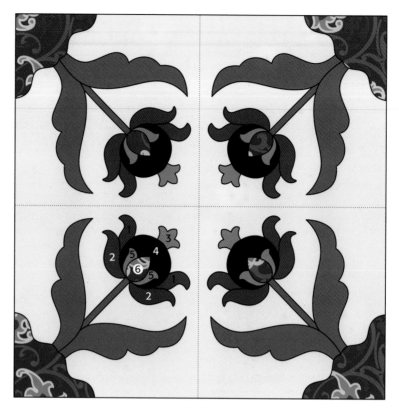

Center Block Diagram

Materials

42"-wide fabric

⅓ yd. green fabric for stems, large leaves, and third
  border
1½ yds. large-scale, multicolored fabric for corner
  brackets, pomegranate centers, and final border
⅓ yd. medium orange fabric for top petals and
  checkerboard border
⅓ yd. bright orange fabric for center petals, finials,
  and checkerboard border
¼ yd. red fabric for pomegranates and first border
½ yd. multicolored accent fabric for bottom petals
  and binding
¾ yd. light background fabric for center block
2¾ yds. of fabric for backing
Batting of your choice, cut 3" larger than quilt top
  on all sides

Center Block

Cutting Chart

Fabrics	Pieces
Green	4 and 4 reversed large leaves
	4 bias strips, each ⅞" x 5¼"
Large-scale, multicolored	4 corner brackets
	4 pomegranate centers
Medium orange	4 and 4 reversed top petals
Bright orange	4 and 4 reversed center petals
	4 finials
Red	4 pomegranates
Multicolored accent	4 and 4 reversed bottom petals
Light background	25" x 25" center block

Appliqué Sequence

1. Prepare the 4 bias stems as shown on page 13.
2. Referring to page 12, trace the appliqué pattern pieces on pages 64–65 onto template material and cut them out.
3. Referring to pages 12–13, trace the templates on the right side of the fabrics and cut out each appliqué.
4. Cut out the center block. Then press horizontal, vertical, and diagonal fold lines into the center block.
5. Following the numerical sequences shown on the center block diagram, half-baste and preconstruct 4 pomegranate units and 4 pomegranate center units. Make sure to clip the seam allowances of all pieces except for edges that will lie underneath other shapes. Refer to the center block diagram to determine where pieces overlap and clipping is not necessary. Leave the tips open on the pomegranate petals.
6. Clip and baste the edges of the large leaves. Leave the tips open so that you can stitch them by needle-turn appliqué later. At the base of the leaves, leave one side unbasted because the reverse leaf will cover this raw edge. The bottoms of the large leaves will be tucked under the corner brackets.

Tuck one seam allowance under and cover with basted edge of other leaf.

7. Baste only the top edge of the 4 corner brackets. The raw edges will lie in the seam allowance of the first border.
8. Position and pin the pomegranate units, large leaves, and corner brackets on the center block. Use the center block diagram as a placement guide. Baste the appliqués in place and remove the pins. Position the 4 bias stems on the diagonally pressed lines in the center block. Baste them in place, tucking the top and bottom of each stem underneath the large leaves and pomegranate units.
9. Appliqué the center block. After the stitching is complete, press and trim the center block to 23½" x 23½".

First Border

1. From the red fabric, cut 2 strips, each 1½" x 23½". Sew these strips to 2 opposite sides of the center block.
2. Cut 2 more red strips, each 1½" x 25½". Sew these strips to the remaining 2 sides of the center block.

Checkerboard Border

Cutting Chart

Fabrics	Pieces
Medium orange	4 strips, each 1½" x 42"
Bright orange	4 strips, each 1½" x 42"

Stitching Sequence

1. Sew 1 medium orange and 1 bright orange strip of fabric together. Make 4 of these strip sets and press the seam allowance toward the darkest fabric. With a rotary cutter and ruler, cut each strip set into 1½" x 2½" units for a total of 108 units.
2. Make 2 checkerboard sections with 25 units in each. Alternate the colors by flipping the units so that the seam allowances butt together. Sew these 2 sections to opposite edges of the first border.
3. Sew 2 more checkerboard sections, each containing 29 units. This will ensure that your color placement is symmetrical on the corners of the checkerboard border. Sew these 2 checkerboard sections to the remaining 2 sides of the first border.

Third Border

1. From the green fabric, cut 2 strips, each 1½" x 30½". Sew these border strips to the top and bottom edges of the checkerboard border.
2. Cut 2 more green strips, each 1½" x 32½". Sew these border strips to the remaining 2 sides of the checkerboard border. Make sure to not stretch the checkerboard border as you stitch.

Final Border

1. From the large-scale, multicolored fabric, cut 2 strips, each 4½" x 32½". Sew these border strips to the top and bottom edges of the third border.
2. Cut 2 more multicolored strips, each 4½" x 40½". Sew these border strips to the remaining 2 sides of the third border.

Quilting and Finishing

1. Prepare the backing with a center seam. Trim the extra fabric from the sides so that backing measures 44" x 44".
2. Layer and baste the backing, batting, and quilt top. Quilt as desired.
3. From the multicolored accent fabric, cut 1½"-wide bias binding strips. You will need enough strips to go around the perimeter of the quilt plus 12" more for corners and overlap. Stitch the binding to the right side of the quilt top; then fold the binding to the back side of the quilt and slipstitch it in place, as shown on pages 26–27.

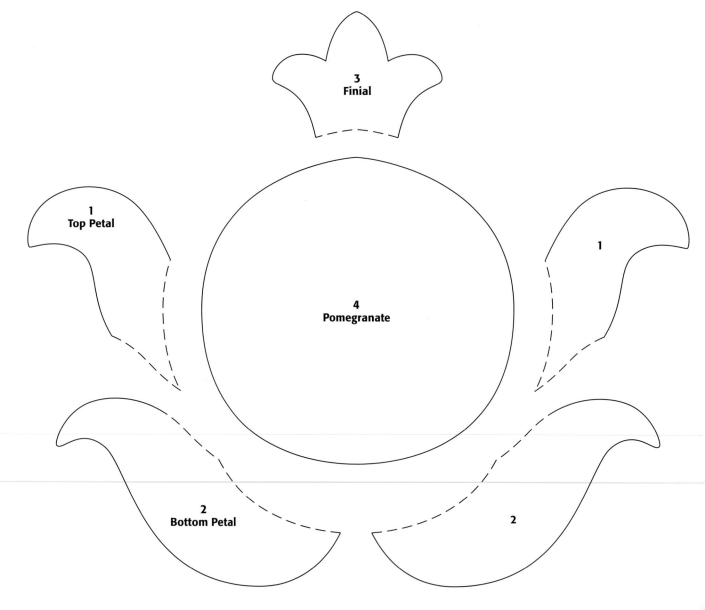

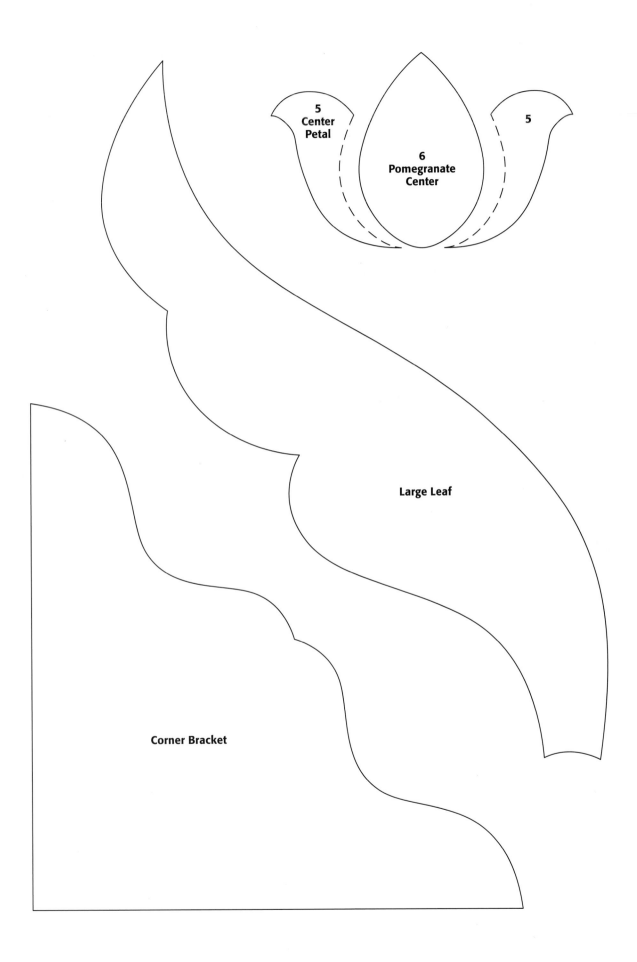

5
Center
Petal

5

6
Pomegranate
Center

Large Leaf

Corner Bracket

FRENCH IRIS WREATH

FRENCH IRIS WREATH
by Sheila Wintle, 1999, Trenholm, Quebec, Canada, 38" x 38".
Almost fleur-de-lys in appearance, the irises in this quilt are quick and
easy to stitch, with a stylized leaf added to accent the lines of the flowers.

CENTER BLOCK ORIENTATION: BASIC WREATH, INWARD

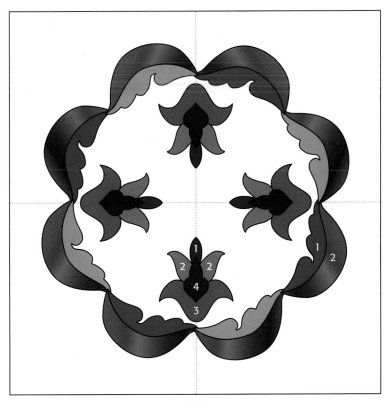

Center Block Diagram

Materials

42"-wide fabric

1¼ yds. multicolored fabric for outer leaves, first border, final border, and binding

1¼ yds. dark blue fabric for inner leaves, final border, and binding

½ yds. bright teal fabric for inner leaves and first borders

⅓ yd. green fabric for iris bases and Sawtooth border

⅓ yd. bright purple fabric for iris petals and Sawtooth border

⅓ yd. dark purple fabric for iris centers and accent borders

Fat quarter of medium purple fabric for iris tops

¾ yd. light background fabric for center block

1¼ yds. of fabric for backing

Batting of your choice, cut 3" larger than quilt top on all sides

Center Block

Cutting Chart

Fabrics	Pieces
Multicolored	8 outer leaves
Dark blue	4 inner leaves
Bright teal	4 inner leaves
Green	4 iris bases
Bright purple	4 and 4 reversed iris petals
Dark purple	4 iris centers
Medium purple	4 iris tops
Light background	25" x 25" center block

Appliqué Sequence

1. Referring to page 13, trace the appliqué pattern pieces on page 70 onto template material and cut them out.
2. Referring to pages 12–13, trace the templates on the right side of the fabrics and cut out each appliqué.
3. Cut out the center block. Then press horizontal, vertical, and diagonal fold lines into the center block.
4. Following the numerical sequence indicated on the pattern pieces, half-baste and preconstruct 4 iris units and 8 leaf units. Leave the tips of each of these pieces open so that you can stitch them with the needle-turn appliqué technique later.
5. Position and pin the iris units and leaf units on the center block. Use the center block diagram as a placement guide. Baste the iris and leaf units on the center block and remove the pins.
6. Appliqué the center block, paying special attention to the area where one leaf unit overlaps the next. Appliqué the end of one leaf unit, overlap it with the tip of the previous leaf, and appliqué that leaf unit in place. After appliquéing the center block, press and trim it to 24" x 24". This center block needs to be trimmed to this size so that the Sawtooth border will fit.

Note: *The fabric in the outer leaves remains the same throughout, but the inner leaves alternate between dark blue and bright teal.*

Leave tip unstitched
until base of next leaf
is attached.

First Border

Cutting Chart

Fabrics	Pieces
Multicolored	2 strips, each 2½" x 28"
Bright teal	2 strips, each 2½" x 28"

Stitching Sequence

1. Position the multicolored border strips on 2 adjacent sides of the center block.
2. Position the bright teal border strips to the remaining 2 adjacent sides of the center block.
3. Sew one of each color border strip to opposite sides of the center block. Start and stop the line of stitching ¼" in from the edge of the quilt top.
4. Sew one of each color border strip to the remaining sides of the quilt top.
5. Miter the corner seams as shown on page 23.

First Accent Border

1. From the dark purple fabric, cut 4 strips, each 1" x 28½".
2. Sew 2 of these accent border strips to opposite sides of the first border. Start and stop the line of stitching ¼" in from the edge of the quilt top. In the same manner, sew the other 2 accent border strips to the remaining sides of the first border.
3. Miter the corner seams as shown on page 23.

Sawtooth Border

1. Referring to "Sawtooth Borders" on pages 21–22 and using the pattern piece on page 70, prepare 116 Sawtooth units from the green and bright purple fabrics.
   Note: *The diagonal strip width will be 2".*
2. Make 4 Sawtooth border sections, each containing 28 Sawtooth units. The direction of the units should reverse at the center of each border section.

Reverse direction of Sawtooth units at center.

3. Sew 2 Sawtooth border sections to the top and bottom edges of the first accent border. Sew one more Sawtooth unit to each end of the 2 remaining Sawtooth sections. These additional units should be positioned so that the purple side of each unit faces the inner edge of the border. This will create 4 symmetrical corners. Sew these 2 Sawtooth border sections to the remaining 2 sides of the first accent border.

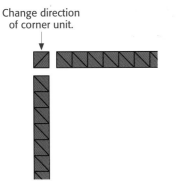

Change direction of corner unit.

Second Accent Border

1. From the dark purple, cut 4 strips, each 1" x 32".
2. Sew 2 of these accent border strips to opposite sides of the Sawtooth border. Start and stop the line of stitching ¼" in from the edge of the quilt top. Sew the other 2 accent border strips to the remaining 2 sides of the Sawtooth border in the same manner.
3. Miter the corner seams as shown on page 23.

Final Border

Cutting Chart

Fabrics	Pieces
Multicolored	2 strips, each 3½" x 39"
Dark blue	2 strips, each 3½" x 39"

Stitching Sequence

1. In the same manner as for the first border section, place the 2 multicolored border strips on adjacent sides of the quilt top. Place the 2 dark blue border strips on the other 2 adjacent sides of the quilt top.
2. Sew 1 of each color border strip to 2 opposite sides of the quilt top. Start and stop each line of stitching ¼" in from the edge of the quilt top.
3. Sew the remaining 2 border strips to the remaining 2 opposite sides of the quilt top. Start and stop each line of stitching ¼" in from the edge of the quilt top.
4. Miter the corner seams as shown on page 23. Trim the mitered seam allowances to ¼" and press them open.

Quilting and Finishing

1. Cut the backing and batting to 42" x 42".
2. Layer and baste the backing, batting, and quilt top. Quilt as desired.
3. The 2-color theme is carried out in the binding of this quilt. From the multicolored fabric and the dark blue fabric, cut 1½"-wide bias strips. You will need enough strips to go around 2 sides of the quilt plus an extra 6" for corners.
4. Starting at a 2-color intersection at one corner of the final border, leave a tail of binding that is 2" long. Using a ⅜" seam allowance, sew the binding strip to the edge of the quilt, make a folded bias corner, and continue sewing the binding to the next side of the quilt. Stop at the next corner. Attach the second color bias-binding strip in the same manner as the first. Follow the instructions on page 23 to miter the corner seams where the 2 colors meet. Trim the ends of the binding tails to reduce bulk in the fold. Fold the binding to the back side of the quilt and slipstitch it in place, as shown on page 27.

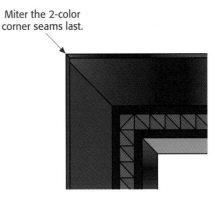

Miter the 2-color corner seams last.

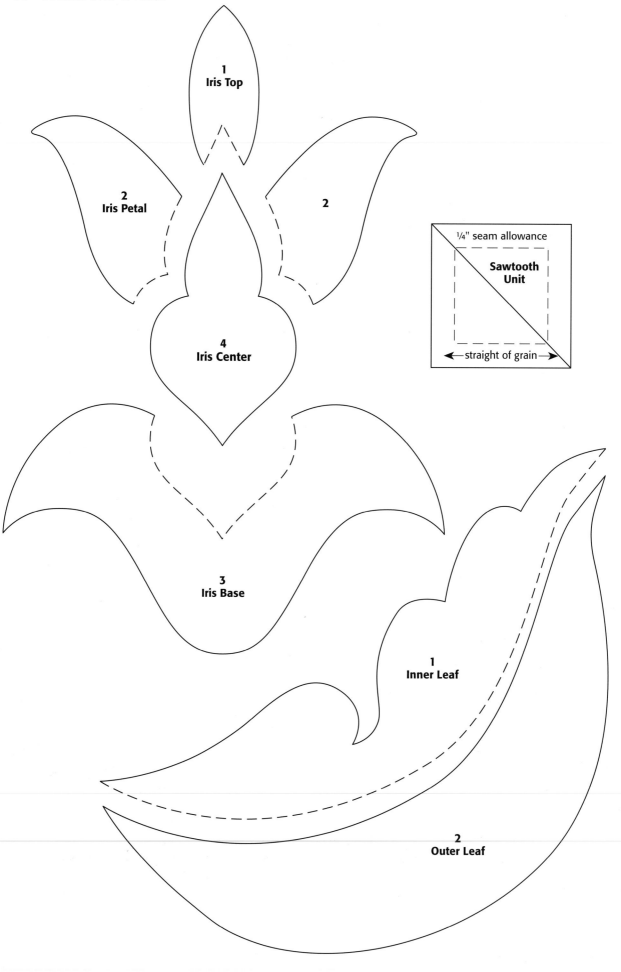

1
Iris Top

2
Iris Petal

2

¼" seam allowance

Sawtooth Unit

← straight of grain →

4
Iris Center

3
Iris Base

1
Inner Leaf

2
Outer Leaf

CIRCLES,
FLOWERS, AND LEAVES

CIRCLES, FLOWERS, AND LEAVES

by Sheila Wintle, 1999, Trenholm, Quebec, Canada, 42" x 42".

This combination of different design elements shows the possibilities that can be achieved with the mix-and-match option. Experiment with your own combinations, and enjoy making great quilts that are one-of-a-kind.

CENTER BLOCK ORIENTATION: DIAMOND, ON-POINT

Center Block Diagram

Materials

42"-wide fabric

½ yd. dark maroon fabric for flower centers, small leaves, medium leaves, stem, setting triangles, and inner border

1½ yds. large-scale, multicolored fabric for flower bases, large leaves, setting triangles, outer border, and binding

⅓ yd. rust fabric for medium leaves, small leaves, flower centers, and setting triangles

¼ yd. each of 2 gold fabrics for small leaves, side leaves, top flower petals, bottom flower petals, and setting triangles

Fat quarter of light purple fabric for large circles, small circles, and setting triangles

¾ yd. light background fabric for center block

2¾ yds. of fabric for backing

Batting of your choice, cut 3" larger than quilt top on all sides

Center Block

Cutting Chart

Fabrics	Pieces
Dark maroon	2 reversed medium leaves
	2 left flower centers
	1 small leaf
	2 bias strips, each ⅞" x 10"
Large-scale, multicolored	2 flower bases
	2 and 2 reversed large leaves
Rust	2 right flower centers
	2 medium leaves
	1 small leaf
First gold	1 and 1 reversed side leaf
	1 reversed small leaf
	2 and 2 reversed top flower petals

Second gold	1 small reversed leaf
	1 and 1 reversed side leaf
	2 and 2 reversed bottom flower petals
Light purple	3 large circles
	6 small circles
Light background	24½" x 24½" center block

Appliqué Sequence

1. Prepare 2 bias stems as shown on page 13.
2. Referring to page 12, trace the appliqué pattern pieces on pages 75–76 onto template material and cut them out.
3. Referring to pages 12–13, trace the templates on the right side of the fabrics and cut out each appliqué.
4. Cut out the center block. Then press diagonal fold lines into the center block.
5. Following the numerical sequence indicated on the center block diagram, half-baste and preconstruct 2 flower units.
6. Clip and baste all of the leaves. Leave the tips and bases open because the bases will be covered by other appliqué pieces. Prepare the large and small circles with the perfect circle technique on pages 13–14. Spray the prepared circles with spray sizing on the wrong sides, and press them to retain the circular shapes. Remove the paper circles just prior to stitching the large and small circles to the background fabric.
7. Referring to the center block diagram, baste the bias stems on the diagonal fold line at the center of the block. Position and pin the flower units and leaves in place. Baste each element to background fabric and remove the pins. Pay special attention to placing the ends of the large and medium leaves under the stem. Use the center block diagram as a placement guide to add the large and small circles.
8. Appliqué the pieces and units to the center block; then press the center block.

Setting Triangles

Cutting Chart

Fabrics	Pieces
Large-scale, multicolored	28 squares, each 4¼" x 4¼". Cut the squares diagonally in one direction to yield 56 half-square triangles.
Dark maroon	8 squares, each 4¼" x 4¼". Cut the squares diagonally in one direction to yield 16 half-square triangles.
Rust	6 squares, each 4¼" x 4¼". Cut the squares diagonally in one direction to yield 12 half-square triangles.
First and second gold	2 squares, each 4¼" x 4¼". Cut the squares diagonally in one direction to yield 4 half-square triangles.
Light purple	4 squares, each 4¼" x 4¼". Cut the squares diagonally in one direction to yield 8 half-square triangles.

Stitching Sequence

1. Measure 3⅞" from the 90° angle of each triangle. Trim each triangle at the 3⅞" marks, as shown.

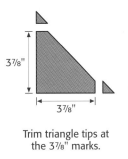

3⅞"

3⅞"

Trim triangle tips at
the 3⅞" marks.

2. Sew the multicolored triangles and the other triangles together into 4 setting triangles. Refer to the diagram for color placements.

Note: *At the corner of each setting triangle, 2 gold triangles form a square.*

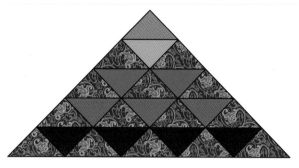

Setting Triangles

3. Refer to the quilt photo on page 71 to sew 1 setting triangle to each side of the center block.

Inner and Outer Borders

Cutting Chart

Fabrics	Pieces
Large-scale, multicolored	4 strips, each 3½" x 43"
Dark maroon	4 strips, each 1¾" x 43"

Stitching Sequence

1. Sew the inner and outer border strips together to form 4 single border sections.
2. Sew the inner and outer border sections to the quilt top, matching the centers. Start and stop each line of stitching ¼" in from the edge of the quilt top.
3. Miter the corner seams as shown on page 23. Trim the mitered seam allowances to ¼" and press them open.

Quilting and Finishing

1. Prepare the backing with a center seam. Trim the extra fabric from the sides so that the backing measures 46" x 46".
2. Layer and baste the backing, batting, and quilt top. Quilt as desired.
3. From the multicolored fabric, cut 1½"-wide bias binding strips. You will need enough strips to go around the perimeter of the quilt plus 12" more for corners and overlap. Stitch the binding to the right side of the quilt top; then fold the binding to the back side of the quilt and slipstitch it in place, as shown on pages 26–27.

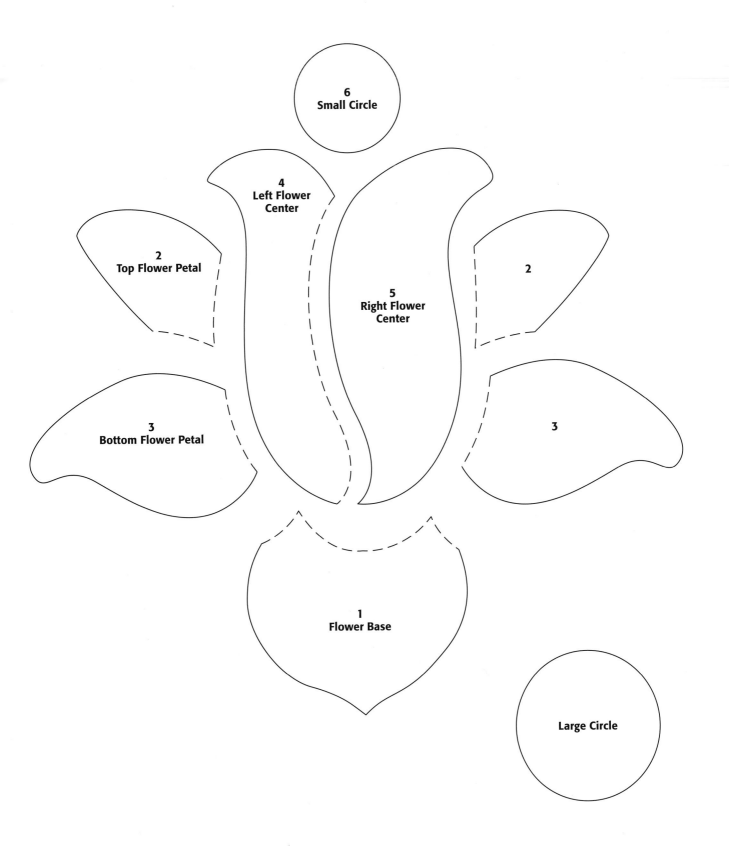

6
Small Circle

4
Left Flower Center

2
Top Flower Petal

2

5
Right Flower Center

3
Bottom Flower Petal

3

1
Flower Base

Large Circle

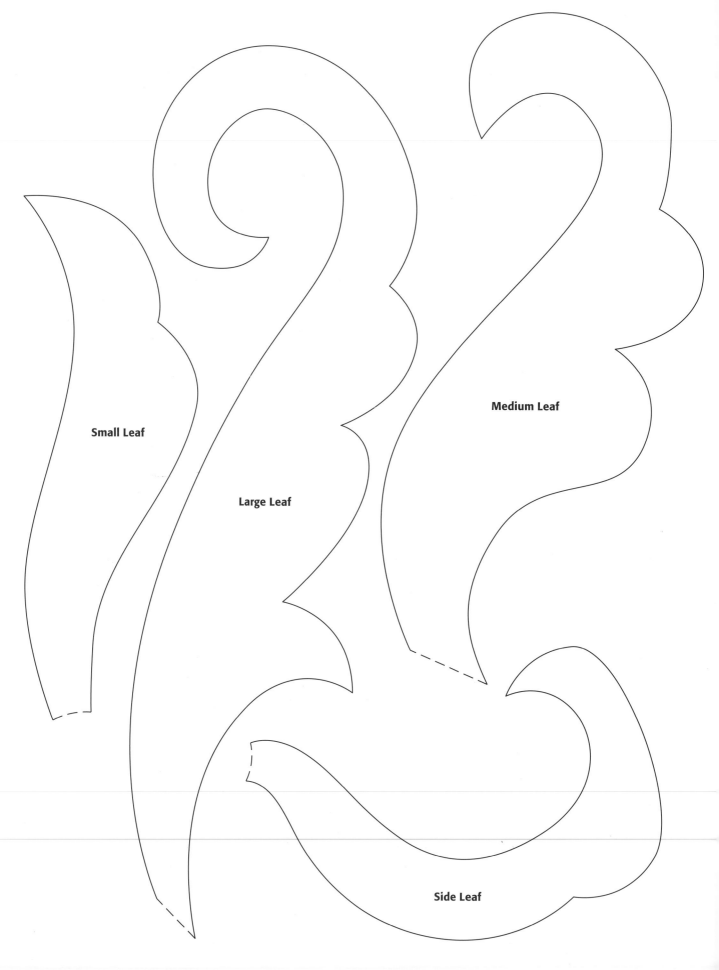

Small Leaf

Large Leaf

Medium Leaf

Side Leaf

FLEUR-DE-LYS

FLEUR-DE-LYS

by Sheila Wintle, 1999, Trenholm, Quebec, Canada, 40" x 40".
Some of the Early American bed ruggs reveal a slight French influence in their designs,
which is echoed in the curved shapes of the tulips and center motif of this quilt.

CENTER BLOCK ORIENTATION: OUTWARD

Center Block Diagram

Materials

42"-wide fabric

⅓ yd. green fabric for stems, circles, and Nine
  Patch blocks
1⅓ yds. multicolored fabric for fleur bases, tulip
  tops, Nine Patch and Star blocks, and final
  border
½ yd. medium blue fabric for fleur tops, center
  motif, Star blocks, and binding
½ yd. light blue fabric for circles and Star blocks
⅓ yd. pink fabric for large tulips and Nine Patch
  blocks
¾ yd. medium background fabric for center block
2½ yds. fabric for backing
Batting of your choice, cut 3" larger than quilt top
  on all sides

Center Block

Cutting Chart

Fabrics	Pieces
Green	4 bias strips, each ⅞" x 5"
	4 circles
Multicolored	4 fleur bases
	4 tulip tops
Medium blue	4 fleur tops
	1 center motif
Light blue	5 circles
Pink	4 large tulips
Medium background	25" x 25" center block

Appliqué Sequence

1. Prepare 4 bias stems as shown on page 13.
2. Referring to page 12, trace the appliqué pattern pieces on pages 80–81 onto template material and cut them out.
3. Referring to pages 12–13, trace the templates on the right side of the fabrics and cut out each appliqué.
4. Cut out the center block. Then press horizontal, vertical, and diagonal fold lines into the center block.
5. Following the numerical sequence indicated on the center block diagram, half-baste and preconstruct 4 fleur units and 4 tulip units. Make sure to clip the seam allowances of all pieces except for the lower edges of the fleur tops.
6. Prepare the circles by using the circle technique shown on pages 13–14. Spray the wrong sides of the gathered circles with sizing to retain the circular shape. Remove the paper just before appliquéing the circles.
7. Using the center block diagram as a placement guide, position, pin, and baste the stems on the diagonally pressed fold lines. Place the center motif over the stems at the center of the block. In the same manner, baste 4 circles at the outermost points of the center motif. Baste the fleur units over the stems at the corners of the block. Baste the tulip units on the horizontal and vertical fold lines next to the 4 circles. Remove the pins.
8. Appliqué the pieces and units to the center block; then press and trim the center block to 24½" x 24½".

Pieced Border

Cutting Chart for Nine Patch Blocks

Fabrics	Pieces
Multicolored	32 squares, each 2½" x 2½"
Pink	24 squares, each 2½" x 2½"
Green	16 squares, each 2½" x 2½"

Cutting Chart for Star Blocks

Fabrics	Pieces
Multicolored	28 squares, each 2⅞" x 2⅞". Cut the squares diagonally in one direction to yield 56 half-square triangles.
Medium blue	8 squares, each 4½" x 4½"
Light blue	20 squares, each 2½" x 2½" 7 squares, each 5¼" x 5¼". Cut the squares diagonally in both directions to yield 28 quarter-square triangles

Stitching Sequence

1. Following the color placements shown, sew the squares for each of the 8 Nine Patch blocks and the pieces for the 8 Star blocks together.

Make 2 top and bottom sections.

Make 2 side sections.

2. Sew 2 top and bottom pieced border sections and 2 side pieced border sections as shown in the previous diagram.
3. Sew the top and bottom sections to the quilt top; then sew the side sections to the quilt top.

Final Border

1. From the multicolored fabric, cut 4 strips, each 2½" x 41".
2. Sew each of these border strips to the edges of the pieced border. Start and stop each line of stitching ¼" in from the edge of the quilt top.
3. Miter the corner seams as shown on page 23.

Quilting and Finishing

1. Prepare the backing with a center seam. Trim the extra fabric from the sides so that the backing measures 44" x 44".
2. Layer and baste the backing, batting, and quilt top. Quilt as desired.
3. From the medium blue fabric, cut 1½"-wide bias binding strips. You will need enough strips to go around the perimeter of the quilt plus 12" more for corners and overlap. Stitch the binding to the right side of the quilt top; then fold the binding to the back side of the quilt and slipstitch it in place, as shown on pages 26–27.

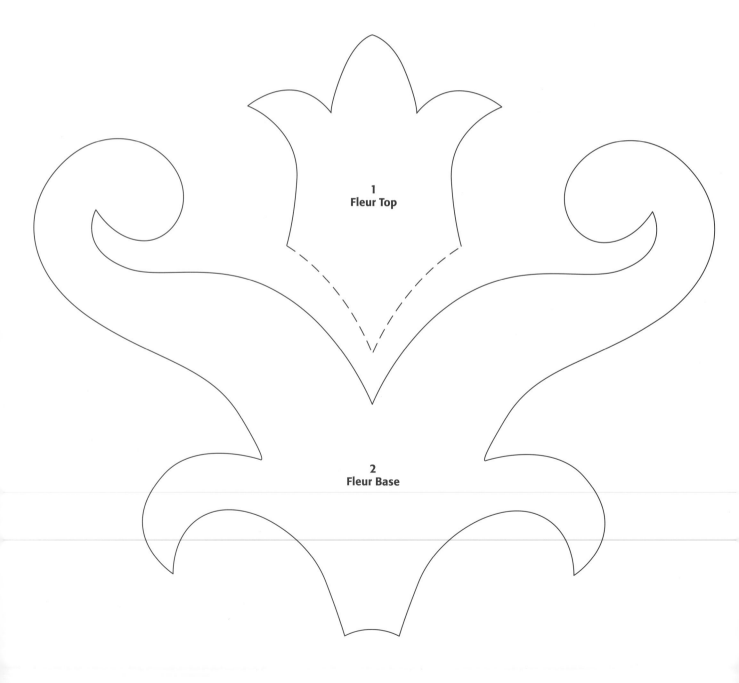

1
Fleur Top

2
Fleur Base

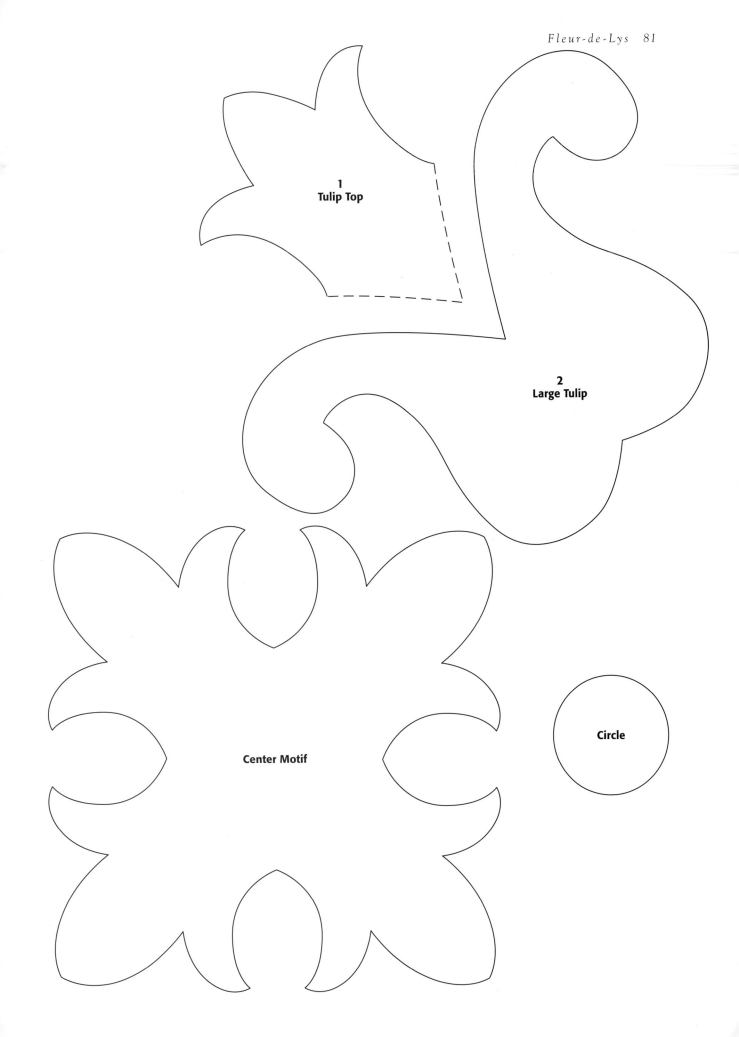

**1
Tulip Top**

**2
Large Tulip**

Center Motif

Circle

COVERLET
TULIPS AND SCROLLS

COVERLET TULIPS AND SCROLLS

by Sheila Wintle, 1999, Trenholm, Quebec, Canada, 40" x 40".
I discovered an embroidered bed rugg that was covered with these lovely tulips. I changed
the design slightly by replacing stems and leaves with these scrolls. This is another
design that lends itself to other combinations with different appliqués.

CENTER BLOCK ORIENTATION: INWARD

Center Block Diagram

Materials

42"-wide fabric

1¼ yds. large-scale, multicolored fabric for scrolls,
final border, and binding

½ yd. rust fabric for upper tulip bases, Nine Patch
border

⅓ yd. teal fabric for lower tulip bases, middle tulip
tops, and third border

¼ yd. fuchsia fabric for upper tulip tops and first
border

Fat quarter of dark purple fabric for lower tulip
tops

1¾ yds. light background fabric for center block
and Nine Patch border

2½ yds. of fabric for backing

Batting of your choice, cut 3" larger than quilt top
on all sides

Center Block

Cutting Chart

Fabrics	Pieces
Large-scale, multicolored	4 and 4 reversed scrolls
Rust	4 and 4 reversed upper tulip bases
Teal	4 and 4 reversed lower tulip bases
	4 middle tulip tops
Fuchsia	4 upper tulip tops
Dark purple	4 lower tulip tops
Light background	25" x 25" center block

Appliqué Sequence

1. Referring to page 13, trace the appliqué pattern pieces on pages 85–86 onto template material and cut them out.
2. Referring to pages 12–13, trace the templates on the right side of the fabrics and cut out each appliqué.
3. Cut out the center block. Then press horizontal, vertical, and diagonal fold lines into the center block.
4. Following the numerical sequence indicated on the center block diagram, half-baste and preconstruct the 4 tulip units. Clip the seam allowances of all pieces except for edges that will lie underneath other shapes. Refer to the center block diagram to determine where pieces overlap and clipping is not necessary.
5. Clip all edges of the scrolls; then turn under the edges and baste. Press the basted scrolls for easy-to-stitch curves. Leave the tips open so that you can stitch them by needle-turn appliqué later.
6. Position, pin, and baste the tulip units on the horizontal and vertical lines at the center of the block. Using the center block diagram as a placement guide, baste the scrolls near the tulip units.
7. Appliqué the units and pieces to the center block; then press and trim the center block to 24½" x 24½".

First Border

1. From the fuchsia fabric, cut 2 strips, each 1¼" x 24½". Sew the strips to the top and bottom edges of the center block.
2. Cut 2 more strips from the fuchsia fabric, each 1¼" x 26". Sew these strips to the sides of the center block.

Nine Patch Border

Cutting Chart

Fabrics	Pieces
Rust	4 strips, each 1½" x 42"
Light background	5 strips, each 1½" x 42"
	10 squares, each 5½" x 5½". Cut the squares diagonally in both directions to yield 40 quarter-square triangles.
	16 squares, each 3⅜" x 3⅜". Cut the squares diagonally in one direction to yield 32 half-square triangles.

Stitching Sequence

1. Sew a rust strip to each side of a light background strip. Repeat for a total of 2 of these strip sets. Press the seam allowances toward the rust fabric. Rotary cut these strip sets into 56 sections, each 1½" x 3½".
2. Sew a light background strip to each side of a rust strip. Rotary cut this strip set into 28 sections, each 1½" x 3½".
3. For each Nine Patch block, sew together 2 sections from step 1 and 1 section from step 2 as shown. Refer to the following diagram to make a total of 28 Nine Patch blocks.

Make 28.

4. Refer to the diagram to sew together 4 border sections. Each section consists of 6 Nine Patch blocks, with quarter-square triangles between them and 2 half-square triangles at each end. Sew 2 of these sections to 2 opposite sides of the first border.

5. Refer to the diagram to sew 4 corner squares that are made with 1 Nine Patch block and 4 half-square triangles on each side. Sew 2 of these corner squares to the ends of the remaining 2 border sections. Sew these 2 border sections to the remaining 2 sides of the first border.

Third Border

1. From the teal fabric, cut 2 strips, each 1¼" x 34½". Sew these strips to 2 opposite sides of the Nine Patch border.
2. Cut 2 more strips, each 1¼" x 36". Sew these strips to the 2 remaining sides of the Nine Patch border.

Final Border

1. From the large-scale, multicolored fabric, cut 4 strips, each 3" x 41".
2. Sew the border strips to each side of the third border. Start and stop each line of stitching ¼" in from the edge of the quilt top.
3. Miter the corner seams as shown on page 23.

Quilting and Finishing

1. Prepare the backing with a center seam. Trim the extra fabric from the sides so that the backing measures 44" x 44".
2. Layer and baste the backing, batting, and quilt top. Quilt as desired.
3. From the multicolored fabric, cut 1½"-wide bias binding strips. You will need enough strips to go around the perimeter of the quilt plus 12" more for corners and overlap. Stitch the binding to the right side of the quilt top; then fold the binding to the back side of the quilt and slipstitch it in place, as shown on pages 26–27.

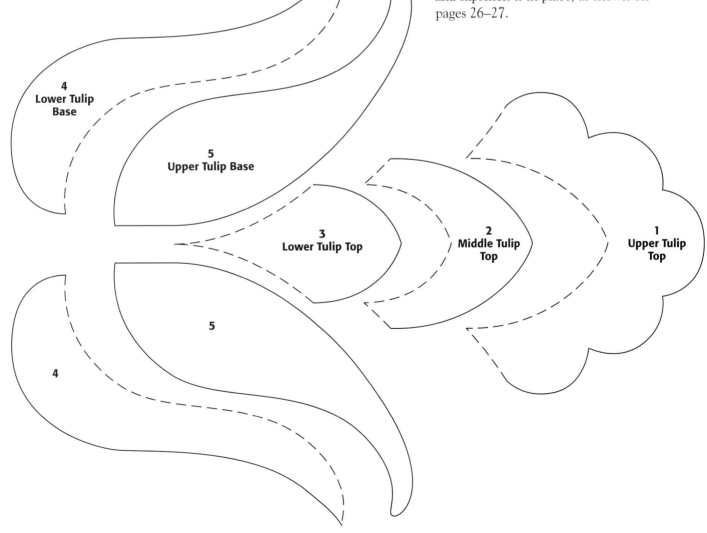

Scroll

FRILLED HEARTS

FRILLED HEARTS

by Sheila Wintle, 1999, Trenholm, Quebec, Canada, 42" x 42".
The large hearts and colorful frills dominate this design. I added the small flowers to the heart centers
for visual interest, and I used them as the focal point for the border treatment.

CENTER BLOCK ORIENTATION: BASIC WREATH

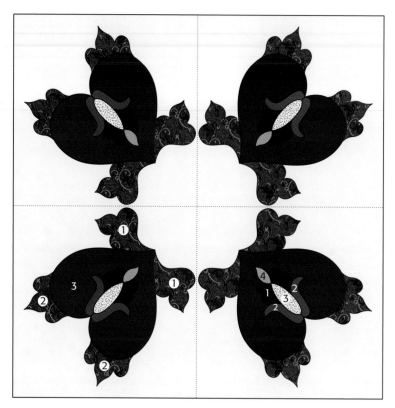

Center Block Diagram

Materials

42"-wide fabric

1⅓ yds. large-scale, multicolored fabric for large top frills, small top frills, bottom frills, final border, and binding

⅔ yds. red fabric for large hearts, small hearts, and flat-edge piping

Fat quarter of green fabric for side petals

Fat quarter of black fabric for flower backs

Fat quarter of white fabric for flower centers

Fat quarter of gold fabric for flower tops and corner squares

1⅝ yds. light background fabric for center block and appliqué border

2¾ yds. of fabric for backing

Batting of your choice, cut 3" larger than quilt top on all sides

Center Block

Cutting Chart

Fabrics	Pieces
Large-scale, multicolored	4 and 4 reversed large top frills
	4 and 4 reversed bottom frills
Red	4 large hearts
Green	4 and 4 reversed side petals
Black	4 flower backs
White	4 flower centers
Gold	4 flower tops
Light background	25" x 25" center block

Appliqué Sequence

1. Referring to page 12, trace the large heart on page 91, the top and bottom frills on page 92, and the flower and petal pieces on page 93 onto template material and cut them out.

2. Referring to pages 12–13, trace the templates on the right side of the fabrics and cut out each appliqué.

3. Cut out the center block. Then press horizontal, vertical, and diagonal fold lines into the center block.

4. Following the numerical sequence shown on the center block diagram, half-baste and preconstruct the heart units and the flower units. Make sure to clip the seam allowances of all pieces except for edges that will lie underneath other shapes. When you get to the deep notch of the heart, clip right down into this area and stop just a few threads away from the marked stitching line, as shown.

TIP: If the fabric you use for the flower centers is very light, you may notice some shadowing from the fabric underneath. If this happens, cut another flower center without any seam allowance and use it as a lining for the flower center.

5. Leave the tips of the large top frills and bottom frills, side petals, and flower tops open so that you can stitch them by needle-turn appliqué later. Baste only the sides of the flower backs because the flower tops will cover the top edge, and the lower edge will be tucked under the side petals and flower center. Position and pin all of the appliqués on the center block.

6. Appliqué the units and pieces to the center block. When the stitching is completed, press and trim the center block to 24½" x 24½".

Appliqué Border

Cutting Chart

Fabrics	Pieces
Red	4 bias strips, each 1½" x 24½"
	4 small hearts
Light background	4 strips, each 6½" x 24½"
Gold	4 squares, each 6½" x 6½"
	8 flower tops
Large-scale, multicolored	4 small top frills
	8 and 8 reversed bottom frills
Green	8 and 8 reversed side petals
Black	8 flower backs
White	8 flower centers

Stitching and Appliqué Sequence

1. Fold the bias strips in half lengthwise and press them to make the flat-edge piping strips. Pin the piping strips along the edges of the center block, aligning raw edges and overlapping the strips at the corners.

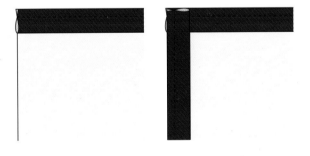

2. Sew a light background strip to 2 opposite sides of the center block. Make sure to encase the piping strips accurately in the seams.

3. Sew a gold square at each end of the remaining 2 light background strips. Sew these 2 strips to the remaining 2 sides of the center block. Encase the piping strips accurately in the seams. The piping strips should overlap neatly at each corner of the center block.

4. Trace, cut out, half-baste, and preconstruct 8 flower units as described in steps 1, 2, and 4 of "Center Block." Leave the tips of the pieces unbasted as described in step 5 of "Center Block."

5. Trace the small heart and small top frill appliqué pattern pieces on page 93 onto template material and cut them out. Trace the templates on the right side of the fabrics and cut out each appliqué.

5. Using the center block diagram and quilt photo as placement guides, position, pin, and baste each flower unit, small heart, and small top frill to the appliqué border. Stitch the appliqués in place.

Final Border

Cutting Chart

Fabrics	Pieces
Red	4 bias strips, each 1½"x 37½"
Large-scale, multicolored	4 strips, each 3½" x 43"

Stitching Sequence

1. Fold the bias strips in half lengthwise and press them to create the flat-edge piping strips. Pin a piping strip to each side of the appliqué border. There is no need to overlap the piping strips at the corners because the corner seams will be mitered.

2. Sew a multicolored strip to each side of the appliqué border. Start and stop each line of stitching ¼" in from the edge of the quilt top. Take care to encase the piping strips in these seams.

3. Miter the corner seams as shown on page 23, encasing the ends of the piping strips in the mitered seam.

Quilting and Finishing

1. Prepare the backing with a center seam. Trim the extra fabric from the sides so that the backing measures 46" x 46".

2. Layer and baste the backing, batting, and quilt top. Quilt as desired.

3. From the multicolored fabric, cut 1½"-wide bias binding strips. You will need enough strips to go around the perimeter of the quilt plus 12" more for corners and overlap. Stitch the binding to the right side of the quilt top; then fold the binding to the back side of the quilt and slipstitch it in place, as shown on pages 26–27.

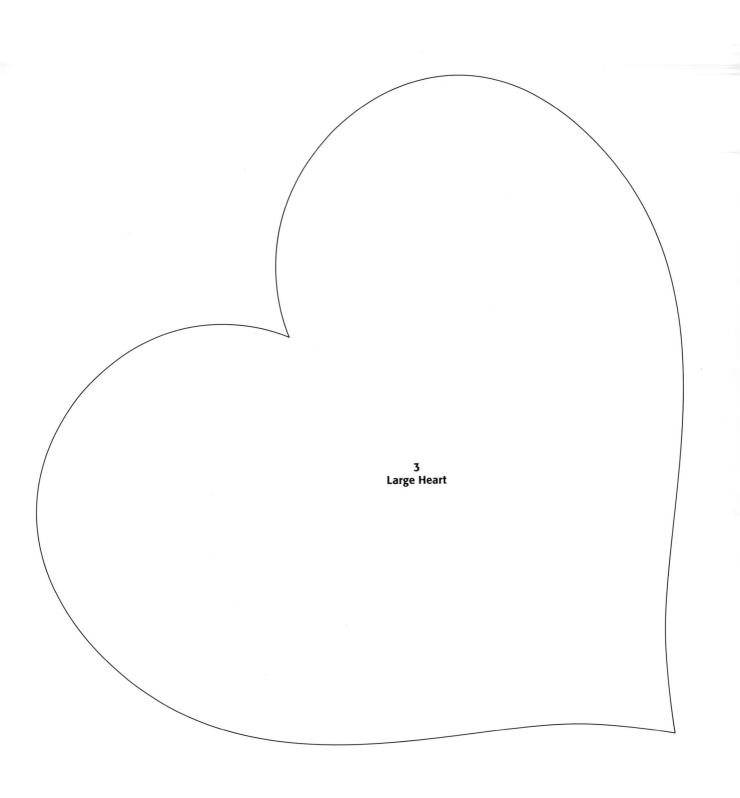

3
Large Heart

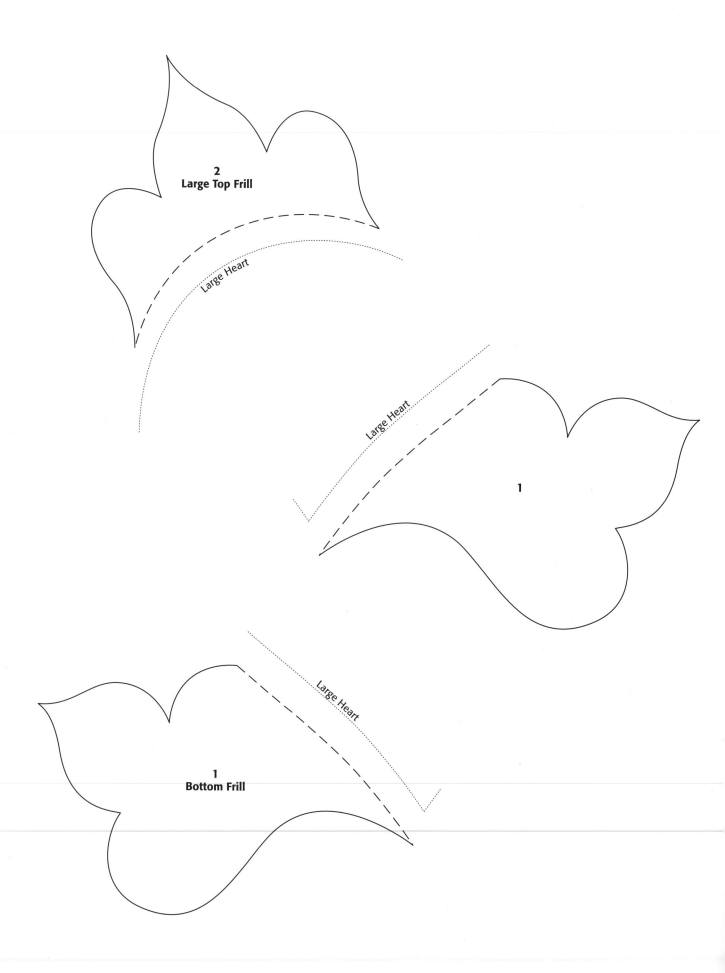

2
Large Top Frill

Large Heart

Large Heart

1

1
Bottom Frill

Large Heart

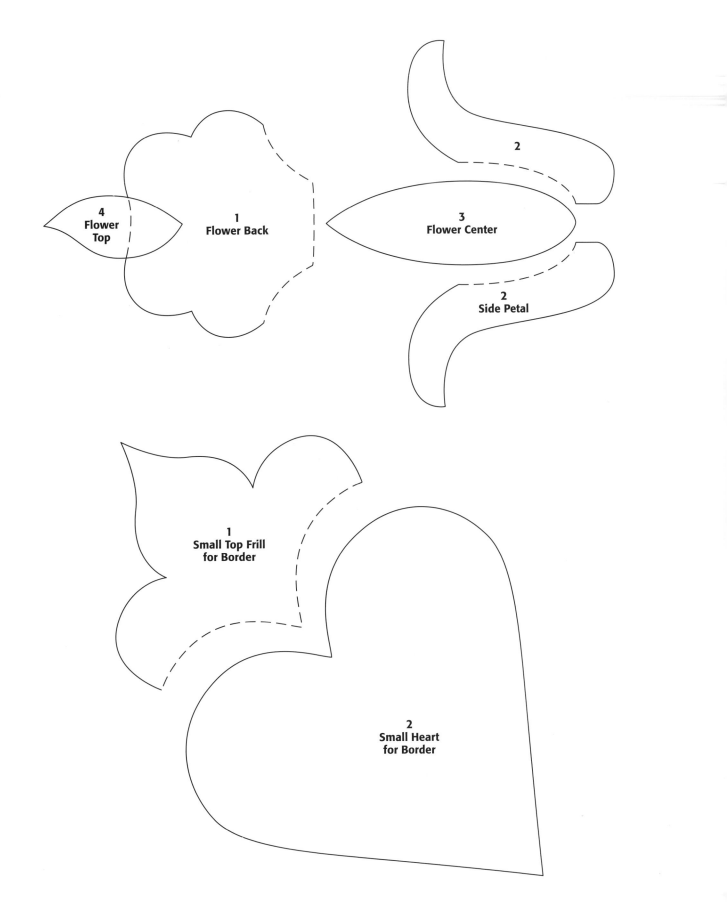

4
**Flower
Top**

1
Flower Back

2

3
Flower Center

2
Side Petal

1
**Small Top Frill
for Border**

2
**Small Heart
for Border**

ASTERS AND DAISIES

ASTERS AND DAISIES
by Sheila Wintle, 1999, Trenholm, Quebec, Canada, 57¼" x 57¼".
Taken from several bed rugg designs and modified to make appliquéing easier, this is a very large design
filled with many motifs. Take the elements you like from this quilt and see how many ways you can mix
and match them with appliqué shapes from other quilts.

CENTER BLOCK ORIENTATION: DIAMOND

Center Block Diagram

Materials

42"-wide fabric

½ yd. light green fabric for aster bases, center base leaf liner, and stems

½ yd. green fabric for outer base leaves and aster leaves

1¾ yds. dark pink fabric for aster petals, bud petals, Dogtooth borders, and binding

Fat quarter of light fabric for daisy petals, center base leaf and liners, daisy leaves, bud bases, and aster leaves

⅓ yd. of medium pink fabric for aster petals, bud petals, outer base leaf liners, center base leaves, and daisy petals

⅓ yd. of dark burgundy fabric for aster petals, bud petals, and circles

2½ yds. dark background fabric for center block, setting triangles, and final border

2 yds. very large-scale, multicolored fabric for Dogtooth borders

3½ yds. of fabric for backing

Batting of your choice, cut 3" larger than quilt top on all sides

Center Block

Cutting Chart

Fabrics	Pieces
Light green	2 aster bases
	1 center base leaf liner
	6 bias strips, each ⅞" x 13"
	2 bias strips, each ⅞" x 2"
Green	1 and 1 reversed outer base leaf
	2 and 2 reversed aster leaves
Dark pink	2 and 2 reversed aster petal #3
	1 and 1 reversed bud petal #3

Cutting chart continued on page 96.

Cutting Chart (Continued)

Fabrics	Pieces
Light	2 each of daisy petal #2, #4, and #6
	1 center base leaf
	2 and 2 reversed daisy leaves
	2 left bud bases
	2 right bud bases
Medium pink	2 and 2 reversed aster petal #2
	2 bud petal #1
	2 bud petal #3
	1 and 1 reversed outer base leaf liner
	2 each of daisy petal #1, #3, #5, and #7
Dark burgundy	3 circles
	2 and 2 reversed aster petal #1
	2 bud petal #2
Dark background	25" x 25" center block

Appliqué Sequence

1. Prepare all of the bias stems as shown on page 13.
2. Referring to page 12, trace the appliqué pattern pieces on pages 99–102 onto template material and cut them out.
3. Referring to pages 12–13, trace the templates on the right side of the fabrics and cut out each appliqué.
4. Cut out the center block. Then press horizontal, vertical, and diagonal fold lines into the center block.
5. Following the numerical sequence indicated on the center block diagram, half-baste and preconstruct 2 daisy units, 2 aster units, and 2 bud units. Make sure to clip the seam allowances of all pieces except for edges that will lie underneath other shapes. Leave the tips of leaves and petals unbasted so that you can stitch them with the needle-turn technique later.

> TIP: If you choose a very dark background fabric, a light box will help you place appliqué shapes more easily.

6. Prepare the circles with the perfect circle technique shown on pages 13–14. Spray the wrong sides of the gathered circles with spray sizing to retain the circular shapes. Remove the paper circles just before you stitch the circles on the background fabric.
7. Using the center block diagram as a placement guide, position, pin, and baste all of the stems in place on the center block. Position and baste the daisy units, aster units, bud units, leaves, and circles on the center block in the same manner.
8. Appliqué the units and pieces to the center block. Add the leaf liners to the leaves and stitch them through all of the layers, to hold the base leaves in place on the background fabric. After the stitching is completed, press and trim the center block to 24½" x 24½".

First Dogtooth Border

Cutting Chart

Fabrics	Pieces
Large-scale, multicolored	48 Dogtooth pieces
	4 and 4 reversed corner Dogtooth pieces
Dark pink	4 and 4 reversed half-Dogtooth pieces
	44 Dogtooth pieces
	4 Dogtooth corner squares
	4 and 4 reversed Dogtooth corner side pieces

Stitching Sequence

1. Using the templates on page 103, sew together 4 Dogtooth sections, each consisting of 12 multicolored Dogtooth pieces and 11 dark pink

Dogtooth pieces, 1 half-Dogtooth piece, and 1 Dogtooth piece reversed, as shown in the diagram. Using the templates on page 103, sew together the 4 corner units for the Dogtooth borders, as shown in the diagram.

Make 4.

Make 4.

2. Sew 1 Dogtooth section to 2 opposite sides of the center block. Sew 1 corner unit to each end of the 2 remaining Dogtooth sections, and sew these sections to the remaining 2 sides of the center block.

Setting Triangles

Cutting Chart

Fabrics	Pieces
Dark background	2 squares, each 23⅞" x 23⅞". Cut the squares diagonally in one direction to yield 4 half-square setting triangles.
Light green	8 bias strips, each ⅞" x 10" 8 aster bases
Dark burgandy	8 and 8 reversed aster petal #1 4 circles
Green	4 and 4 reversed outer base leaves

Medium pink	4 and 4 reversed outer base leaf liners 4 center base leaves 8 and 8 reversed aster petal #3
Dark pink	8 and 8 reversed aster petal #2
Light	8 and 8 reversed aster leaves 4 center base leaf liners

Stitching and Appliqué Sequence

1. Sew 2 setting triangles to 2 opposite sides of the center block.
2. Sew the remaining 2 setting triangles to the remaining 2 sides of the center block.
3. Prepare the 8 bias stems as shown on page 13. Position and baste the bias stems on the setting triangles.
4. Prepare the circles with the perfect circle technique shown on pages 13–14. Spray the wrong sides of the gathered circles with spray sizing to retain the circular shapes. Remove the paper circles just before you stitch the circles on the background fabric.
5. Trace, cut out, half-baste, and preconstruct 4 base leaf units and 8 aster units. Refer to steps 2, 3, 5, 7, and 8 in "Center Block" for additional guidance. Position and baste the appliqué units and circles on the setting triangles.
6. Appliqué the units and pieces to the setting triangles. After the stitching is completed, press and trim the setting triangles so that the quilt top measures 46½" x 46½".

Second Dogtooth Border

Cutting Chart

Fabrics	Pieces
Large-scale, multicolored	92 Dogtooth pieces 4 and 4 reversed corner Dogtooth pieces
Dark pink	88 Dogtooth pieces 4 and 4 reversed half-Dogtooth pieces 4 Dogtooth corner squares 4 and 4 reversed corner side Dogtooth pieces

Stitching Sequence

1. Sew together 4 Dogtooth sections, each containing 23 multicolored Dogtooth pieces, 22 dark pink Dogtooth pieces, 1 pink half-Dogtooth piece and 1 pink half-Dogtooth piece reversed, in the same manner as for the first Dogtooth border. Using the templates on page 103, sew together the 4 corner units for the Dogtooth borders, in the same manner as before.

2. Sew 1 Dogtooth section to 2 opposite sides of the quilt top. Sew 1 corner unit to each end of the 2 remaining Dogtooth sections, and sew these sections to the remaining 2 sides of the quilt top.

Final Border

1. From the dark background fabric, cut 4 strips, each 2½" x 59".
2. Sew the 4 final border strips to the edges of the second Dogtooth border. Start and stop the stitching lines ¼" in from the edges of the quilt top.
3. Miter the corner seams as shown on page 23.

Quilting and Finishing

1. Prepare the backing with a center seam. Trim the extra fabric from the sides so that the backing measures 60" x 60".
2. Layer and baste the backing, batting, and quilt top. Quilt as desired.
3. From the dark pink fabric, cut 1½"-wide bias binding strips. You will need enough strips to go around the perimeter of the quilt plus 12" more for corners and overlap. Stitch the binding to the right side of the quilt top; then fold the binding to the back side of the quilt and slipstitch it in place, as shown on pages 26–27.

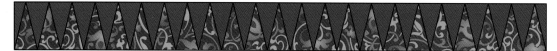

Make 4.

Make 4.

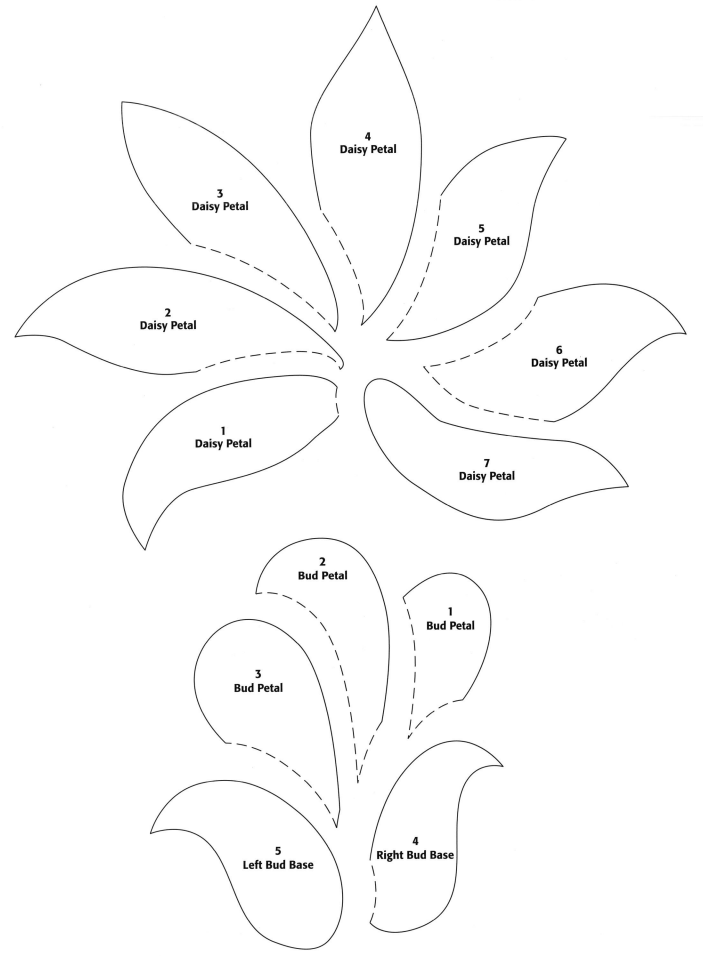

4
Daisy Petal

3
Daisy Petal

5
Daisy Petal

2
Daisy Petal

6
Daisy Petal

1
Daisy Petal

7
Daisy Petal

2
Bud Petal

1
Bud Petal

3
Bud Petal

5
Left Bud Base

4
Right Bud Base

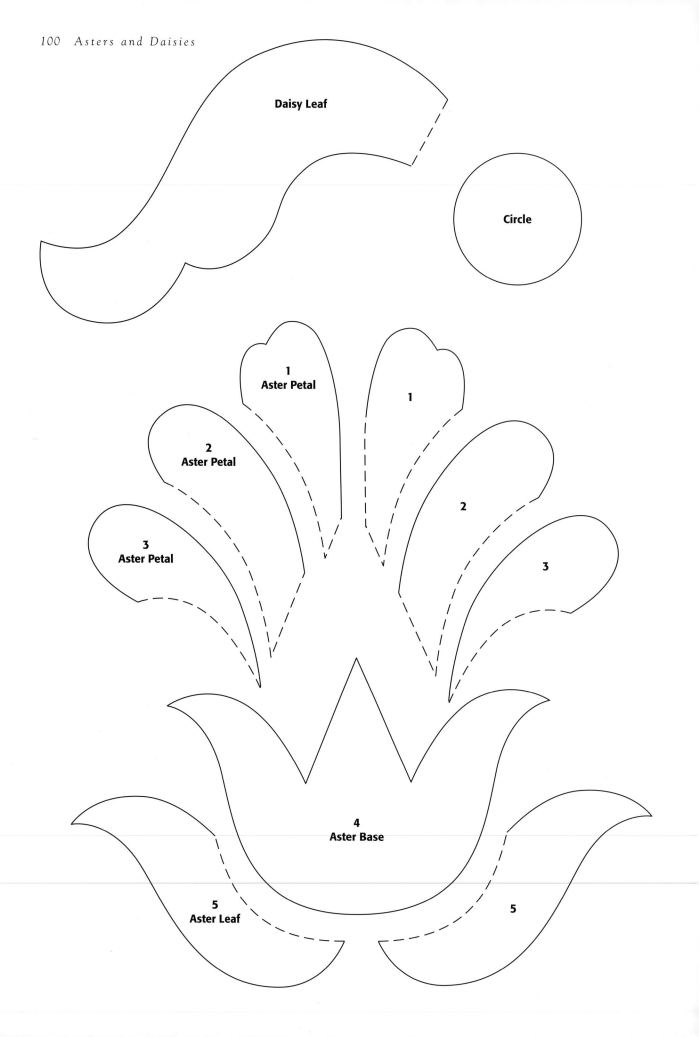

Daisy Leaf

Circle

1
Aster Petal

1

2
Aster Petal

2

3
Aster Petal

3

4
Aster Base

5
Aster Leaf

5

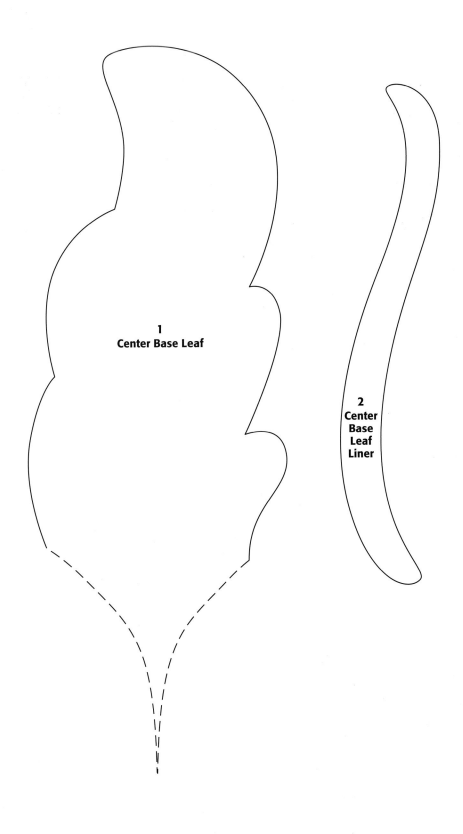

**1
Center Base Leaf**

**2
Center
Base
Leaf
Liner**

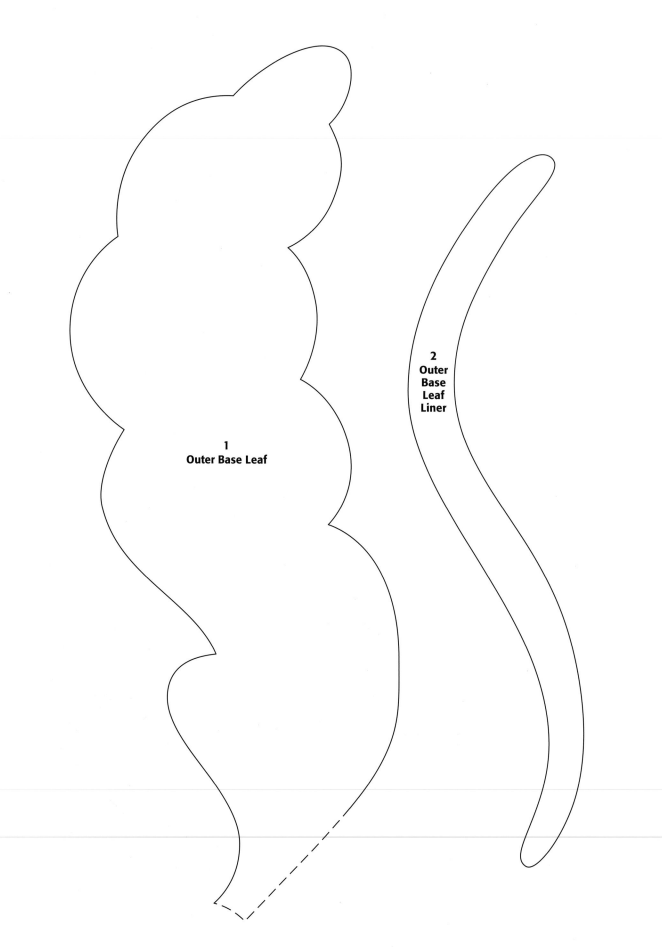

**1
Outer Base Leaf**

**2
Outer
Base
Leaf
Liner**

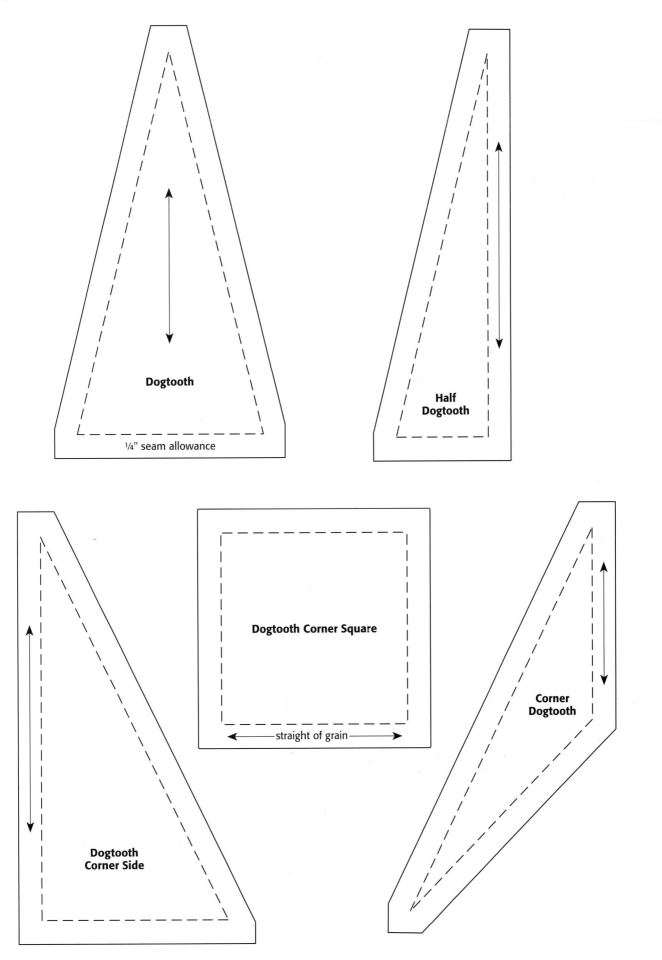

Dogtooth

¼" seam allowance

Half Dogtooth

Dogtooth Corner Side

Dogtooth Corner Square

straight of grain

Corner Dogtooth

HIGH STYLE

HIGH STYLE

by Sheila Wintle, 1999, Trenholm, Quebec, Canada, 42" x 42".
This small, squatty vase is a classic bed rugg design, which I wanted to interpret in today's colors.
The appliqué detail from the vase is echoed in the corners of the pieced border.

CENTER BLOCK ORIENTATION: OUTWARD

Center Block Diagram

Materials

42"-wide fabric

Fat quarter each of 2 green fabrics for large leaf tops, medium leaves, side leaves, stems, and second border squares

1½ yds. large-scale, multicolored fabric for large leaf bottoms, vase leaves and base motif, side flower leaves, first border, final border, and binding

½ yd. light pink fabric for side flower backs, top flower center, and first border

⅓ yd. dark blue fabric for top flower leaves, circles, and third border

¼ yd. tan fabric for the vase, vase handle, and second border

Fat quarter of dark pink fabric for top flower back, vase circle, and vase leaves

Fat quarter of bright pink fabric for side flower centers and third border corner squares

Fat quarter of light blue fabric for circles and top flower base

¾ yd. light background fabric for center block

2¾ yds. of fabric for backing fabric

Batting of your choice, cut 3" larger than quilt top on all sides

Center Block

Cutting Chart

Fabrics	Pieces
First and second greens	1 and 1 reversed large leaf top
	1 and 1 reversed medium leaf
	1 and 1 reversed side leaf
	3 bias strips, each ⅞" x 10"
Light background	25" x 25" center block
Large-scale, multicolored	1 and 1 reversed large leaf bottom
	2 and 2 reversed side flower leaves
	1 and 1 reversed vase leaf
	1 base motif

Cutting chart continued on page 106.

Cutting Chart (Continued)

Fabrics	Pieces
Light pink	2 side flower backs
	1 top flower center
Dark blue	3 circles
	1 top flower leaves
Tan	1 vase
	1 and 1 reversed vase handle
Dark pink	1 top flower back
	1 circle
Bright pink	2 side flower centers
Light blue	2 circles
	1 top flower base

Appliqué Sequence

1. Prepare the 3 bias stems as shown on page 13.
2. Referring to page 12, trace the appliqué pattern pieces on pages 108–111 onto template material and cut them out.
3. Referring to pages 12–13, trace the templates on the right side of the fabrics and cut out each appliqué.
4. Cut out the center block. Then press horizontal, vertical, and diagonal fold lines into the center block.
5. Following the numerical sequence indicated on the center block diagram, half-baste and preconstruct 2 side flower units, 1 top flower unit, 1 vase unit, and 2 large leaf units. Make sure to clip the seam allowances of the leaves and baste the edges. Leave the tips of the leaves unbasted so that you can stitch them by needle-turn appliqué later.
6. Prepare the circles using the perfect circle technique on pages 13–14. Spray the wrong sides of the gathered circles with sizing to retain the circular shape. Remove the paper circles just before stitching the circles to the background fabric.
7. Using the center block diagram as a placement guide, baste the stems, flower units, leaf units, vase unit, and circles on the center block.
8. Appliqué the units and pieces to the center block. After the stitching is complete, press and trim the center block to 24½" x 24½".

First Border

Cutting Chart

Fabrics	Pieces
Large-scale, multicolored	4 squares, each 7¼" x 7¼". Cut the squares diagonally in both directions to yield 16 quarter-square triangles.
Light pink	5 squares, each 7¼" x 7¼". Cut the squares diagonally in both directions to yield 20 quarter-square triangles.
Dark pink	4 and 4 reversed vase leaves
Dark blue	4 circles

Stitching and Appliqué Sequence

1. Make 4 border sections, each containing 4 multi-colored triangles and 3 light pink triangles, as shown. Sew one of these border sections to each side of the center block, as shown.

2. Sew together 2 light pink triangles for each corner of the first border. Sew the pieced triangles to each corner of the pieced border.

3. Trace and cut out 4 circles. Prepare the circles using the perfect circle technique on pages 13–14. Spray the wrong sides of the gathered circles with spray sizing to retain the circular shape.
4. Following the numerical sequence indicated on the center block vase unit, half-baste and pre-construct 4 first border leaf units. Each leaf unit consists of 1 and 1 reversed vase leaf and a circle. Stitch the units to the corners of the first border. Use the photo on page 104 as a placement guide.

Second Border

Cutting Chart

Fabrics	Pieces
Tan	4 strips, each 1½" x 30¼"
Green	4 squares, each 1½" x 1½"

Stitching Sequence

1. Sew 2 tan strips to 2 opposite sides of the first border.
2. Sew a green 1½" square to each end of the remaining 2 tan strips. Sew these border strips to the remaining 2 opposite edges of the first border.

Third Border

Cutting Chart

Fabrics	Pieces
Dark blue	4 strips, each 2½" x 32"
Bright pink	4 squares, each 2½" x 2½"

Stitching Sequence

1. Sew 2 dark blue strips to 2 opposite sides of the second border.
2. Sew a bright pink 2½" square to each end of the remaining dark blue strips. Sew these border strips to the remaining 2 opposite edges of the second border.

Final Border

1. From the large-scale, multicolored fabric, cut 4 strips, each 3½" x 43".
2. Sew the border strips to the quilt top. Start and stop the lines of stitching ¼" in from the edges of the quilt top.
3. Miter the corner seams as shown on page 23.

Quilting and Finishing

1. Prepare the backing with a center seam. Trim the extra fabric from the sides so that the backing measures 46" x 46".
2. Layer and baste the backing, batting, and quilt top. Quilt as desired.
3. From the multicolored fabric, cut 1½"-wide bias binding strips. You will need enough strips to go around the perimeter of the quilt plus 12" more for corners and overlap. Stitch the binding to the right side of the quilt top; then fold the binding to the back side of the quilt and slipstitch it in place, as shown on pages 26–27.

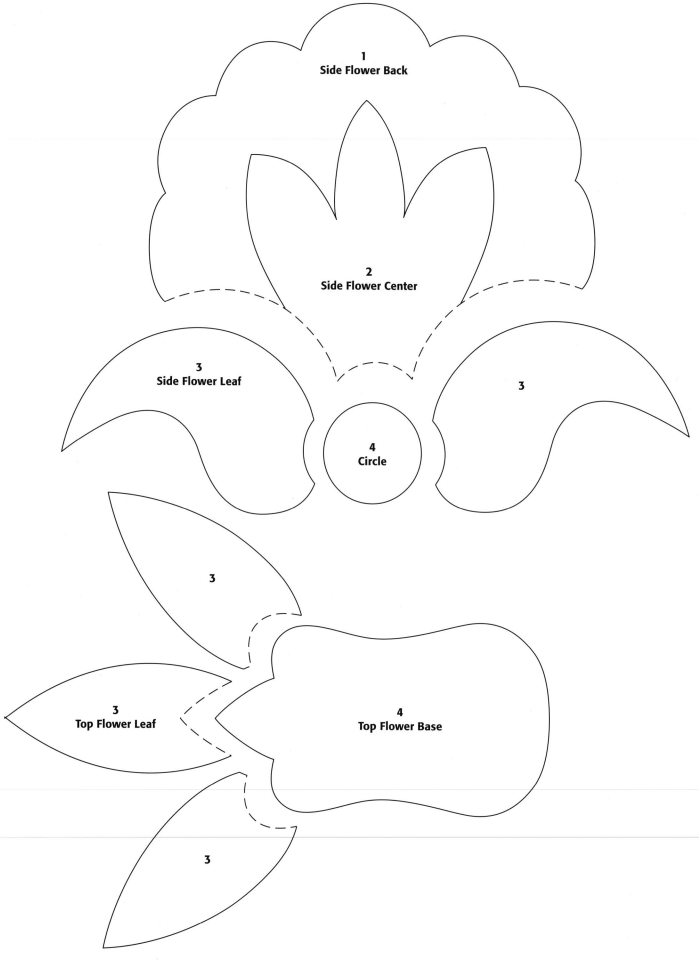

1
Side Flower Back

2
Side Flower Center

3
Side Flower Leaf

3

4
Circle

3

3
Top Flower Leaf

4
Top Flower Base

3

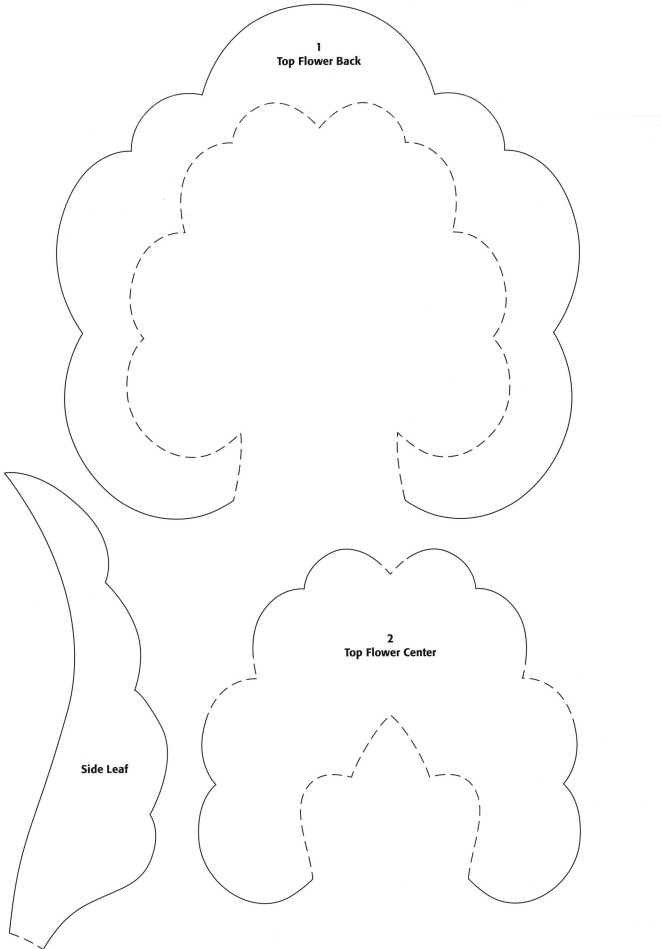

1
Top Flower Back

2
Top Flower Center

Side Leaf

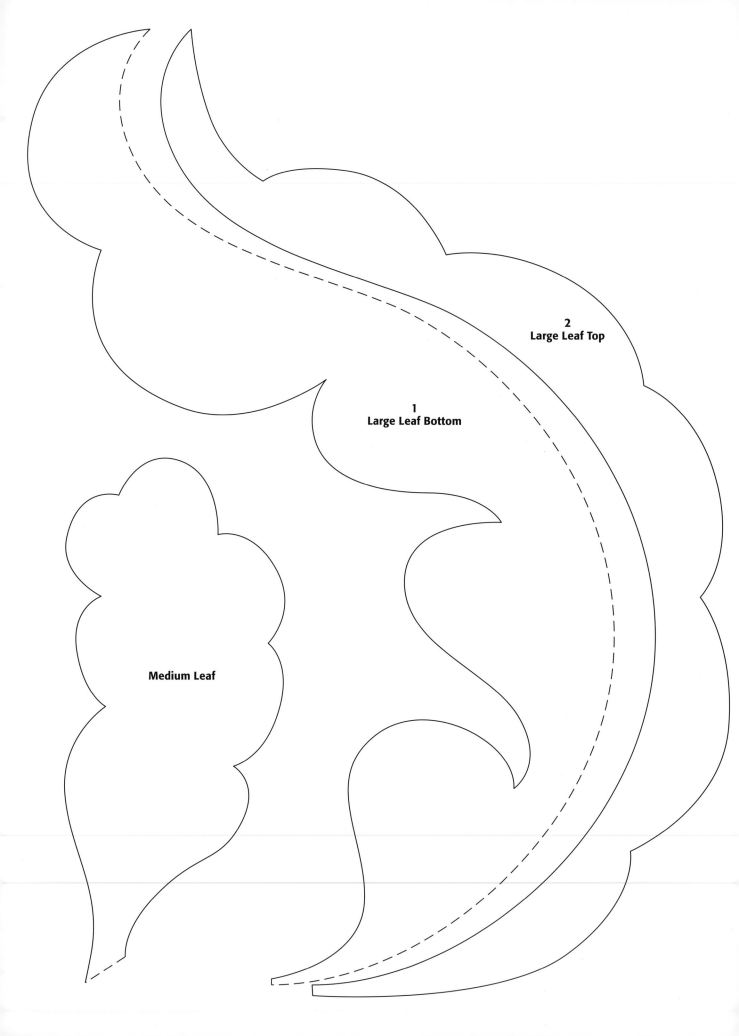

2
Large Leaf Top

1
Large Leaf Bottom

Medium Leaf

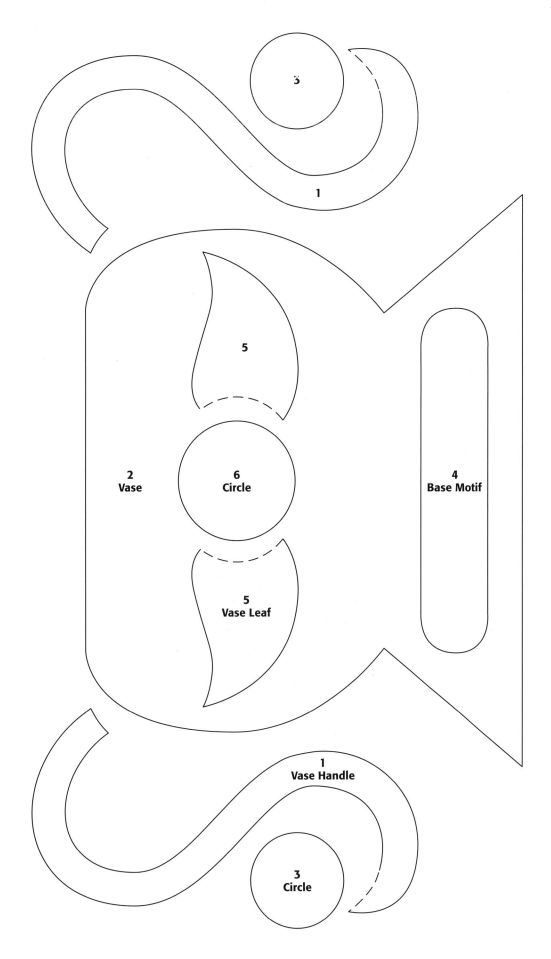

3

1

5

2
Vase

6
Circle

4
Base Motif

5
Vase Leaf

1
Vase Handle

3
Circle

RESOURCES

Houck, Carter. *American Quilts and How to Make Them*. New York: Charles Scribners, 1975.

McKim, Ruby. *101 Patchwork Patterns*. New York: Dover Publications, 1962.

ABOUT
THE AUTHOR

Sheila Wintle learned to quilt during the quilting revival of 1976. Living in an area devoid of quilting supplies, she found it difficult at first. After completing her first quilt, however, she knew there would be many more to follow. Sheila began teaching adult-education classes and discovered she had a talent for teaching and loved sharing her quiltmaking skills with others.

Quiltmaking has opened the doors to the world of color and design for Sheila and has given her the opportunity to teach many interesting quilters. She encourages her students to follow their instincts. She tells them, "You are here to learn, and my purpose is not to turn out a clone of me but to empower you to do your own thing." Sheila lives with her parents and other family members on the family dairy farm in the Eastern Townships of Quebec. Sheila and her mother started their own custom-quiltmaking business, and they enjoy quilting together every day.

Sheila is a two-time Best of Show winner at the Vermont Quilt Festival, as well as an award winner at the American Quilters Society Show in Paducah, Kentucky. In 1998, she was a finalist at the International Quilt Association Show in Houston, Texas.